MW00462664

ALL-TIME
AMERICAN
FAVORITES

ALL-TIME

AMERICAN FAVORITES

*Over 100 step-by-step recipes, with over
400 color photographs*

FRANCES CLEARY

ANNESS
PUBLISHING

This edition published 1995

© Anness Publishing Limited 1995

ISBN 0-8317-2759-4

Editorial Director: Joanna Lorenz
Project Editor: Carole Clements
Copy Editor: Norma MacMillan
Designer: Sheila Volpe
Photographer: Amanda Heywood
Food Styling: Frances Cleary, Carole Handslip,
steps by Nicola Fowler

Printed and bound in Singapore

CONTENTS

~

SOUPS, SANDWICHES & APPETIZERS   6

FISH & SEAFOOD   28

MEAT & POULTRY   42

SALADS, VEGETABLES, EGGS & CHEESE   64

BREADS, CAKES, PIES & COOKIES   90

HOT & COLD DESSERTS   110

INDEX   127

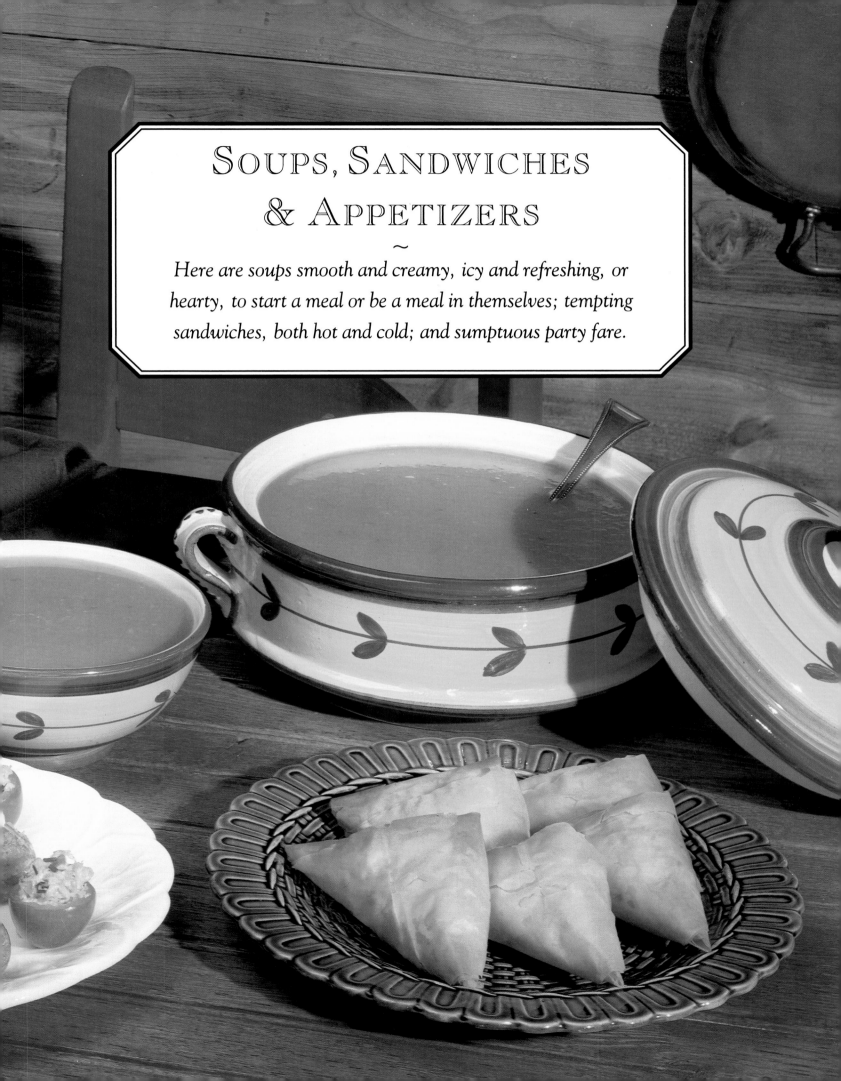

SOUPS, SANDWICHES & APPETIZERS

~

Here are soups smooth and creamy, icy and refreshing, or hearty, to start a meal or be a meal in themselves; tempting sandwiches, both hot and cold; and sumptuous party fare.

Winter Vegetable Soup

SERVES 8

1 medium-size head of Savoy cabbage, quartered and cored

2 tablespoons corn oil

4 carrots, thinly sliced

2 celery stalks, thinly sliced

2 parsnips, diced

6 cups chicken stock

3 medium-size potatoes, diced

2 zucchini, sliced

1 small red bell pepper, seeded and diced

2 cups cauliflower florets

2 tomatoes, seeded and diced

½ teaspoon fresh thyme leaves or ¼ teaspoon dried thyme

2 tablespoons chopped fresh parsley

salt and pepper

1 Slice the cabbage quarters into thin strips across the leaves.

2 ▲ Heat the oil in a large saucepan. Add the cabbage, carrots, celery, and parsnips and cook 10–15 minutes over medium heat, stirring frequently.

3 Stir the stock into the vegetables and bring to a boil. Skim off any foam that rises to the top.

4 ▲ Add the potatoes, zucchini, bell pepper, cauliflower and tomatoes with the herbs, and salt and pepper to taste. Bring back to a boil. Reduce the heat to low, cover the pan, and simmer until the vegetables are tender, 15–20 minutes.

Fresh Tomato Soup

SERVES 4

2 tablespoons butter or margarine

1 onion, chopped

2 pounds tomatoes, quartered

2 carrots, chopped

2 cups chicken stock

2 tablespoons chopped fresh parsley

½ teaspoon fresh thyme leaves or ¼ teaspoon dried thyme

⅓ cup whipping cream (optional)

salt and pepper

~ **COOK'S TIP** ~

Meaty and flavorful Italian plum tomatoes are ideal for this soup.

1 Melt the butter or margarine in a large saucepan. Add the onion and cook until softened, about 5 minutes.

2 ▲ Stir in the tomatoes, carrots, chicken stock, parsley and thyme. Bring to a boil. Reduce the heat to low, cover the pan, and simmer until tender, 15–20 minutes.

3 ▼ Purée the soup in a vegetable mill. Return the puréed soup to the saucepan.

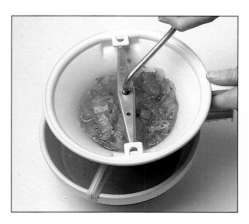

4 Stir in the cream, if using, and reheat gently. Season with salt and pepper. Ladle into warmed soup bowls and serve hot, sprinkled with a little more thyme, if you wish.

Winter Vegetable Soup (top), Fresh Tomato soup

Chilled Avocado and Zucchini Soup

SERVES 6

4 cups chicken stock

1 pound zucchini, sliced

2 large, very ripe avocados

3 tablespoons fresh lemon juice

¾ cup plain yogurt

2 teaspoons Worcestershire sauce

½ teaspoon chili powder

⅛ teaspoon sugar

dash of hot pepper sauce

salt

1 In a large saucepan, bring the chicken stock to a boil.

2 ▲ Add the zucchini and simmer until soft, 10–15 minutes. Let cool.

3 ▲ Peel the avocados. Remove and discard the pits. Cut the flesh into chunks and put in a food processor or blender. Add the lemon juice and process until smooth.

4 ▲ Using a slotted spoon, transfer the zucchini to the food processor or blender; reserve the stock. Process the zucchini with the avocado purée.

5 ▲ Pour the avocado-zucchini purée into a bowl. Stir in the reserved stock. Add ½ cup of the yogurt, the Worcestershire sauce, chili powder, sugar, hot pepper sauce, and salt to taste. Mix well. Cover tightly and chill 3–4 hours.

6 To serve, ladle the soup into bowls. Swirl the remaining yogurt on the surface.

Chicken Noodle Soup

SERVES 8

1 3-pound chicken, cut in pieces
2 onions, quartered
1 parsnip, quartered
2 carrots, quartered
½ teaspoon salt
1 bay leaf
2 allspice berries
4 black peppercorns
3 quarts water
1 cup very thin egg noodles
sprigs of fresh dill, for garnishing

1 ▲ In a large stockpot, combine the chicken pieces, onions, parsnip, carrots, salt, bay leaf, allspice berries and peppercorns.

2 ▲ Add the water to the pot and bring to a boil, skimming frequently.

3 Reduce the heat to low and simmer 1½ hours, skimming occasionally.

4 Strain the broth through a fine-mesh strainer into a bowl. Refrigerate overnight.

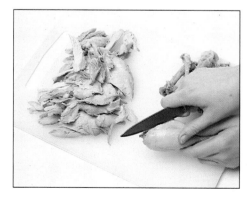

5 ▲ When the chicken pieces are cool enough to handle, remove the meat from the bones. Discard the bones, skin, vegetables, and flavorings. Chop the chicken meat and refrigerate overnight.

6 Remove the solidified fat from the surface of the chilled broth. Pour the broth into a saucepan and bring to a boil. Taste the broth; if a more concentrated flavor is wanted, boil 10 minutes to reduce slightly.

7 ▲ Add the chicken meat and noodles to the broth and cook until the noodles are tender, about 8 minutes (check package directions for timing). Serve hot, garnished with dill sprigs.

Green Bean and Parmesan Soup

SERVES 4

2 tablespoons butter or margarine

½ pound green beans, trimmed

1 garlic clove, minced

2 cups vegetable stock

salt and pepper

½ cup freshly grated Parmesan cheese

¼ cup light cream

2 tablespoons chopped fresh parsley

1 Melt the butter or margarine in a medium saucepan. Add the green beans and garlic and cook 2–3 minutes over medium heat, stirring frequently.

2 ▲ Stir in the stock and season with salt and pepper. Bring to a boil. Reduce the heat and simmer, uncovered, until the beans are tender, 10–15 minutes.

3 ▼ Pour the soup into a blender or food processor and process until smooth. Alternatively, purée the soup in a food mill. Return to the pan. Stir in the cheese and cream. Sprinkle with the parsley and serve.

Hearty Lentil Soup

SERVES 6

1 cup brown lentils

4 cups chicken stock

1 cup water

¼ cup dry red wine

1½ pounds ripe tomatoes, peeled, seeded, and chopped, or 2 cups canned crushed tomatoes

1 carrot, sliced

1 onion, chopped

1 celery stalk, sliced

1 garlic clove, minced

¼ teaspoon ground coriander

2 teaspoons chopped fresh basil, or ½ teaspoon dried basil

1 bay leaf

6 tablespoons freshly grated Parmesan cheese

1 ▲ Rinse the lentils and discard any discolored ones and any stones.

2 ▲ Combine the lentils, stock, water, wine, tomatoes, carrot, onion, celery, and garlic in a large saucepan. Add the coriander, basil, and bay leaf.

3 ▼ Bring to a boil, reduce the heat to low, cover, and simmer until the lentils are just tender, 20–25 minutes, stirring occasionally.

4 Discard the bay leaf. Ladle the soup into 6 soup bowls and sprinkle each with 1 tablespoon of the cheese.

~ VARIATION ~

For a more substantial soup, add about 1 cup finely chopped cooked ham for the last 10 minutes of cooking.

Green Bean and Parmesan Soup (top), Hearty Lentil Soup

Mozzarella, Tomato, and Pesto Sandwiches

SERVES 4

4 small round Italian or French bread rolls

½ cup freshly made or bottled pesto sauce

½ pound mozzarella cheese, thinly sliced

4 medium tomatoes, thinly sliced

3 tablespoons olive oil

fresh basil leaves, for garnishing

1 With a serrated knife, cut each roll open in half. Spread 1 tablespoon of pesto sauce over the cut side of each half.

2 ▲ Arrange alternating slices of mozzarella cheese and tomato on the bottom half of each roll.

3 ▲ Drizzle the olive oil over the cheese and tomatoes.

4 Replace the top half of each roll; garnish with basil leaves, if you wish.

Salad-Stuffed Pita Pockets

SERVES 6

½ small head of iceberg lettuce, cut in fine strips across the leaves

½ hothouse cucumber, diced

9 cherry tomatoes, halved

2 scallions, finely chopped

½ cup crumbled feta cheese

8 black olives, pitted and chopped

6 oblong pita breads, cut in half crosswise

FOR THE DRESSING

1 small garlic clove, minced

⅛ teaspoon salt

1 teaspoon fresh lemon juice

2 tablespoons olive oil

1 teaspoon chopped fresh mint

pepper

1 ▲ In a bowl, combine the lettuce, cucumber, tomatoes, scallions, feta cheese, and olives.

2 ▲ For the dressing, combine all the ingredients in a small screwtop jar and shake well to mix.

3 ▲ Pour the dressing over the salad and toss together.

4 ▲ Gently open the pita bread halves. Fill the pockets with the salad. Serve immediately.

Mozzarella, Tomato and Pesto Sandwiches (top), Salad-Stuffed Pita Pockets

Club Sandwiches

SERVES 4

8 bacon slices

12 slices of white bread or rectangular brioche, toasted

½ cup mayonnaise

¼–½ pound cooked chicken breast meat, sliced

8 large lettuce leaves

salt and pepper

1 beefsteak tomato, cut across in 4 slices

1 ▼ In a heavy skillet, fry the bacon until crisp and the fat is rendered. Drain on paper towels.

2 Lay 4 slices of toast on a flat surface. Spread them with some of the mayonnaise.

3 ▲ Top each slice with one-quarter of the chicken and a lettuce leaf. Season with salt and pepper.

4 ▲ Spread 4 of the remaining toast slices with mayonnaise. Lay them on top of the lettuce.

5 ▲ Top each sandwich with a slice of tomato, 2 bacon slices, and another lettuce leaf.

6 Spread the remaining slices of toast with the rest of the mayonnaise. Place them on top of the sandwiches, mayonnaise-side down.

7 Cut each sandwich into four triangles and secure each triangle with a toothpick.

Chili Dogs

SERVES 6

6 frankfurters

6 hot dog buns, split open

2 tablespoons butter or margarine, at room temperature

⅓ cup shredded cheddar cheese

⅓ cup chopped red onion

FOR THE CHILI

2 tablespoons corn oil

1 small onion, chopped

1 small green bell pepper, seeded and chopped

½ pound ground beef

1 cup tomato sauce

½ cup drained canned red kidney beans

2 teaspoons chili powder, or to taste

salt and pepper

3 ▼ Stir in the tomato sauce, beans, chili powder, and salt and pepper to taste. Cover the pan and simmer 10 minutes.

4 Meanwhile, put the frankfurters in a saucepan and cover with cold water. Bring to a boil. Remove from the heat, cover, and let stand 5 minutes.

5 ▲ Spread both sides of each hot dog bun with the butter or margarine. Fry in a hot skillet until golden brown on both sides.

6 To serve, put a frankfurter in each bun. Top with chili and sprinkle with cheese and onion. Serve immediately.

1 ▲ For the chili, heat the oil in a skillet. Add the onion and green bell pepper and cook until softened, about 5 minutes.

2 ▲ Add the beef and cook until well browned, stirring frequently and breaking up lumps with the side of a wooden spatula.

Spinach and Feta Phyllo Triangles

SERVES 20

2 tablespoons olive oil
2 shallots, finely chopped
1 pound frozen spinach, thawed
¼ pound feta cheese, crumbled
⅓ cup walnut pieces, chopped
¼ teaspoon grated nutmeg
salt and pepper
4 large or 8 small sheets phyllo pastry
½ cup (1 stick) butter or margarine, melted

1 Preheat the oven to 400°F.

2 ▲ Heat the olive oil in a skillet. Add the shallots and cook until softened, about 5 minutes.

3 ▲ A handful at a time, squeeze all the liquid out of the spinach. Add the spinach to the shallots. Increase the heat to high and cook, stirring, until all excess moisture has evaporated, about 5 minutes.

4 ▲ Transfer the spinach mixture to a bowl. Let cool. Stir in the feta and walnuts. Season with nutmeg, salt and pepper.

5 ▲ Lay a phyllo sheet on a flat surface. (Keep the remaining phyllo covered with a damp cloth to prevent it drying out.) Brush with some of the butter or margarine. Lay a second phyllo sheet on top of the first. With scissors, cut the layered phyllo pastry lengthwise into 3-inch-wide strips.

~ VARIATION ~

For an alternative filling, omit the spinach and shallots. Use ¾ pound goat cheese, crumbled, instead of the feta cheese, and ½ cup toasted pine nuts instead of the walnuts. Mix the cheese with the olive oil and 1 tablespoon chopped fresh basil. Assemble as above.

6 ▲ Place a tablespoonful of the spinach mixture at the end of one strip of phyllo pastry.

7 ▲ Fold a bottom corner of the pastry over the filling to form a triangle, then continue folding over the pastry strip to the other end. Fill and shape the triangles until all the ingredients are used.

8 ▲ Set the triangles on baking sheets and brush with butter. Bake the phyllo triangles until they are crispy and golden brown, about 10 minutes. Serve hot.

Cornmeal and Smoked Salmon Muffins

Makes 25

½ cup cornmeal

¼ cup flour

½ teaspoon baking powder

⅛ teaspoon salt

1 tablespoon sugar

1 egg

½ cup buttermilk

¼ cup light cream

½ cup smoked salmon, cut in fine strips

1 Preheat the oven to 400°F. Grease a mini-muffin tray.

2 In a mixing bowl, combine the cornmeal, flour, baking powder, salt, and sugar. Set aside.

3 ▼ In another bowl, mix together the egg, buttermilk, and cream. Gradually add the egg mixture to the cornmeal mixture, stirring quickly until just combined.

4 ▲ Stir the smoked salmon strips into the batter.

5 Fill the mini-muffin pans three-quarters full with the batter. Bake until slightly risen and golden brown, 18–20 minutes. Let cool 5 minutes in the pans on a wire rack before unmolding.

Black Bean and Tomato Salsa in Corncups

Makes 30

1 15-ounce can black (turtle) beans, rinsed and drained

2 tomatoes, seeded and diced

1 garlic clove, minced

1 shallot, minced

1 jalapeño pepper, seeded and chopped

1 teaspoon finely grated lime rind

1 tablespoon olive oil

2 tablespoons fresh lime juice

2 teaspoons maple syrup

salt and pepper

3 tablespoons chopped fresh coriander (cilantro)

For the corncups

10 6-inch corn tortillas

3–4 tablespoons corn oil, for brushing

1 Preheat the oven to 400°F.

2 ▼ For the corncups, using a 2-inch round cookie cutter, cut 3 rounds from each tortilla, pressing firmly to cut through. Discard the tortilla trimmings. Brush both sides of each tortilla round with oil.

3 Press the tortilla rounds into the cups of 2–3 mini-muffin trays. Bake until the corncups are crisp, about 6 minutes. Let cool on a wire rack.

4 ▲ In a mixing bowl, combine the beans, tomatoes, garlic, shallot, jalapeño, lime rind, oil, lime juice, and maple syrup. Stir in salt and pepper to taste.

5 Place a spoonful of the bean and tomato salsa in each corncup. Sprinkle with the chopped coriander just before serving.

Cornmeal and Smoked Salmon Muffins (top), Black Bean and Tomato Salsa in Corncups

Potato Pancakes with Lemon-Chive Cream

Makes 40

2 tablespoons butter or margarine
1 shallot, finely chopped
1 egg
½ pound potatoes
oil for frying
For the lemon-chive cream
½ cup cream cheese, at room temperature
2 tablespoons sour cream
1 teaspoon finely grated lemon rind
1 tablespoon fresh lemon juice
1 tablespoon chopped fresh chives

1 Melt the butter or margarine in a small skillet. Add the shallot and cook until softened, about 3 minutes. Set aside and let cool.

2 Beat the egg in a large mixing bowl until light and frothy.

3 Coarsely grate the potatoes. Add them to the bowl and mix with the egg until completely coated. Season generously with salt and pepper. Add the shallot and mix well.

4 ▼ For the lemon-chive cream, combine the cream cheese and sour cream in a bowl. Beat until smooth. Add the lemon rind and juice and chives. Set aside.

5 ▲ Heat ¼ inch of oil in a skillet. Drop teaspoonfuls of the potato mixture into the hot oil and press them with the back of a spoon to make flat rounds. Fry until well browned, 2–3 minutes on each side. Drain on paper towels and keep warm while frying the remaining pancakes.

6 Serve the pancakes hot, with the lemon-chive cream for spooning on top, or for dipping.

Crab-Stuffed Cherry Tomatoes

Makes 40

¼ pound lump crab meat
1 teaspoon chili sauce
¼ teaspoon Dijon-style mustard
2 tablespoons mayonnaise
½ teaspoon Worcestershire sauce
2 scallions, finely chopped
1 tablespoon chopped fresh basil
1 tablespoon chopped fresh chives
40 cherry tomatoes
salt

1 In a mixing bowl, combine the crab meat, chili sauce, mustard, mayonnaise, Worcestershire sauce, scallions, and herbs. Mix well. Cover and refrigerate until needed.

2 ▲ Using a serrated knife, cut a very thin slice from the stem end of each tomato. Carefully scoop out the pulp and seeds with the tip of a teaspoon.

3 Sprinkle the insides of the tomato shells lightly with salt. Invert them on paper towels and let them drain 15 minutes.

4 ▲ Using a small spoon, stuff the tomatoes with the crab, mounding the filling slightly on top. Serve cold.

Potato Pancakes with Lemon-Chive Cream (top), Crab-Stuffed Cherry Tomatoes

Corn and Garlic Fritters

SERVES 4

5 garlic cloves

3 eggs, beaten

¾ cup flour

salt and pepper

¾ cup fresh corn kernels, or drained canned corn or frozen corn, thawed

1 cup sour cream

2 tablespoons chopped fresh chives

3 tablespoons corn oil

1 Preheat the broiler.

2 Thread the garlic cloves onto a skewer. Broil close to the heat, turning, until charred and soft. Let cool.

3 ▼ Peel the garlic cloves. Place them in a bowl and mash with a fork. Add the eggs, flour, and salt and pepper to taste and stir until well mixed. Stir in the corn. Set aside for at least 30 minutes.

4 In a small bowl, combine the sour cream and chives. Cover and refrigerate.

5 ▲ To cook the fritters, heat the oil in a frying pan. Drop in spoonfuls of the batter and fry until lightly browned on both sides, about 2 minutes, turning once. Drain on paper towels.

6 Serve the fritters hot with the chive cream.

Cheese and Mushroom Frittata

SERVES 4

2 tablespoons olive oil

2 cups small mushrooms, sliced

3 scallions, finely chopped

6 eggs

1 cup shredded cheddar cheese

1 tablespoon chopped fresh dill or ¼ teaspoon dried dill

salt and pepper

1 Heat the oil in a heavy 8-inch skillet, preferably with an ovenproof handle. Add the mushrooms and scallions and cook over medium heat until wilted, about 3 minutes, stirring occasionally.

2 ▲ Break the eggs into a bowl and beat to mix. Add the cheese, dill, and salt and pepper to taste.

3 Preheat the broiler.

4 ▼ Spread the vegetables evenly in the skillet. Pour the egg mixture into the skillet. Cook until the frittata is set at the edge, and the underside is golden, 5–6 minutes.

5 Place the skillet under the broiler, about 3 inches from the heat. Broil until the top of the frittata has set and is lightly browned, 3–4 minutes. Transfer to a warmed platter for serving.

Corn and Garlic Fritters (top), Cheese and Mushroom Frittata

Baby Baked Potatoes with Blue Cheese Topping

MAKES 20

20 small new potatoes

¼ cup vegetable oil

coarse salt

½ cup sour cream

¼ cup crumbled blue cheese

2 tablespoons chopped fresh chives

1 Preheat the oven to 350°F.

2 Wash and dry the potatoes. Pour the oil into a bowl. Add the potatoes and toss to coat well with oil.

3 ▼ Dip the potatoes in the coarse salt to coat lightly. Spread out the potatoes on a baking sheet. Bake until tender, 45–50 minutes.

4 ▲ In a small bowl, combine the sour cream and blue cheese.

5 ▲ Cut a cross in the top of each potato. Press with your fingers to open the potatoes.

6 ▲ Top each potato with a dollop of the cheese mixture. Sprinkle with chives and serve immediately.

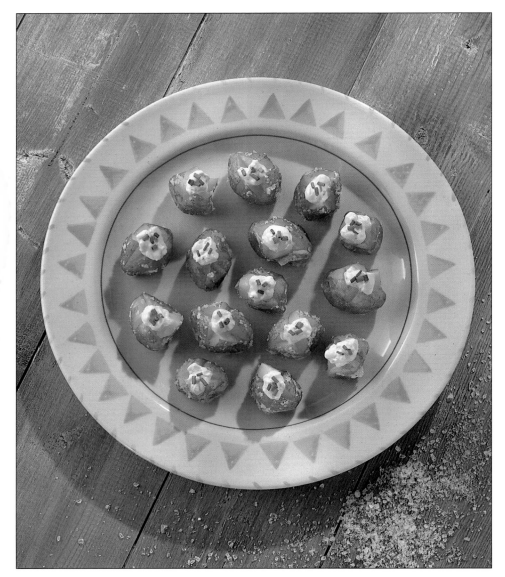

Guacamole with Cumin Tortilla Chips

SERVES 10

2 very ripe avocados

2 shallots or scallions, chopped

2 tablespoons fresh lime juice

1 teaspoon salt

2 teaspoons chili powder

1 medium-size tomato, seeded and chopped

FOR THE CUMIN TORTILLA CHIPS

3 tablespoons corn oil

1½ teaspoons ground cumin

1 teaspoon salt

9 6-inch corn tortillas, each cut in 6 triangles

1 Preheat the oven to 300°F.

2 ▲ For the tortilla chips, combine the oil, cumin, and salt in a bowl.

3 ▲ Spread the tortilla triangles on 2 baking sheets. Brush the seasoned oil on both sides. Bake until they are crisp and golden, about 20 minutes, turning once or twice and brushing with the seasoned oil. Let cool.

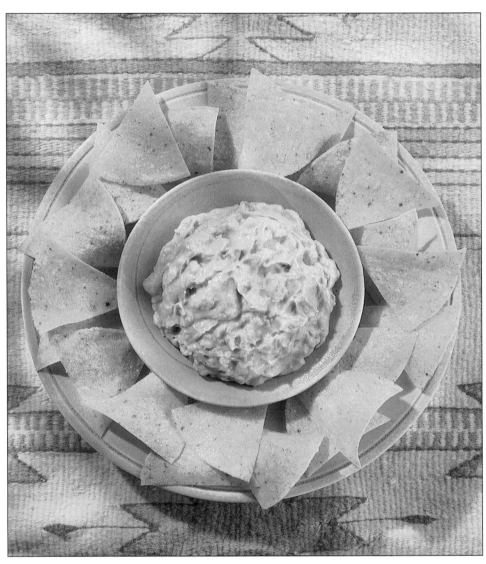

4 ▼ Peel the avocados, discard the pits, and chop the flesh. In a food processor or blender, combine the avocados, shallots or scallions, lime juice, salt, and chili powder. Process until smooth.

5 ▲ Transfer the mixture to a bowl. Gently stir in the chopped tomato.

6 Serve the guacamole in a bowl in the center of a platter, surrounded with the cumin tortilla chips.

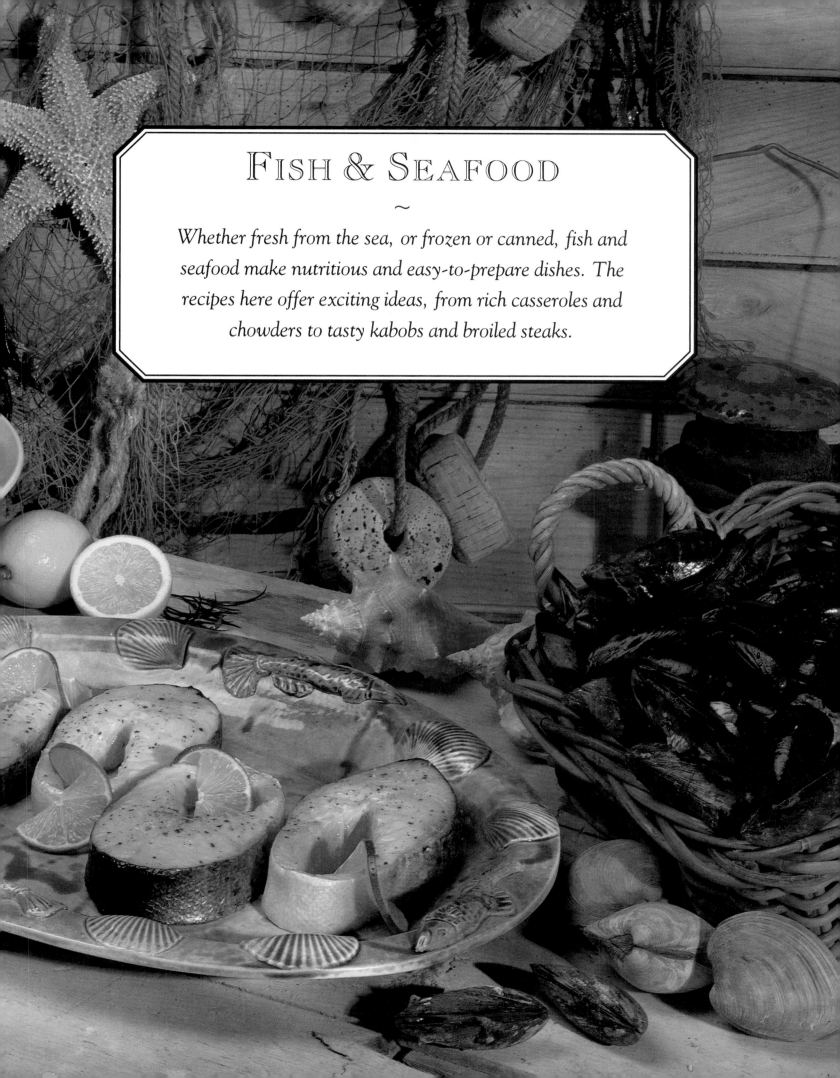

FISH & SEAFOOD

~

*Whether fresh from the sea, or frozen or canned, fish and
seafood make nutritious and easy-to-prepare dishes. The
recipes here offer exciting ideas, from rich casseroles and
chowders to tasty kabobs and broiled steaks.*

Breaded Fish with Tartare Sauce

SERVES 4

½ cup dry bread crumbs

1 teaspoon dried oregano

½ teaspoon cayenne

1 cup milk

2 teaspoons salt

4 pieces of cod fillet (about 1½ pounds)

3 tablespoons butter or margarine, melted

FOR THE TARTARE SAUCE

½ cup mayonnaise

½ teaspoon Dijon-style mustard

1 kosher dill pickle spear, finely chopped

1 tablespoon drained capers, chopped

1 teaspoon chopped fresh parsley

1 teaspoon chopped fresh chives

1 teaspoon chopped fresh tarragon

salt and pepper

1 Preheat the oven to 450°F. Grease a shallow glass or porcelain baking dish.

2 ▲ Combine the bread crumbs, oregano, and cayenne on a plate and blend together. Mix the milk with the salt in a bowl, stirring well to dissolve the salt.

3 ▲ Dip the pieces of cod fillet in the milk, then transfer to the plate and coat with the bread crumb mixture.

4 ▲ Arrange the coated fish in the prepared baking dish, in one layer. Drizzle the melted butter or margarine over the fish.

5 Bake until the fish flakes easily when tested with a fork, 10–15 minutes.

6 ▲ Meanwhile, for the tartare sauce, combine all the ingredients in a small bowl. Stir gently to mix well.

7 Serve the fish hot, accompanied by the tartare sauce.

Stuffed Sole Rolls

SERVES 4

8 skinless sole fillets (about 1 pound)
1 tablespoon butter or margarine, cut in 8 pieces
¼ cup dry white wine
paprika, for garnishing
FOR THE STUFFING
2 tablespoons butter or margarine
1 small onion, finely chopped
1 handful of fresh spinach leaves, shredded (1 cup firmly packed)
2 tablespoons pine nuts, toasted
2 tablespoons raisins
2 tablespoons fresh bread crumbs
⅛ teaspoon ground cinnamon
salt and pepper

1 Preheat the oven to 400°F. Butter a shallow baking dish.

2 ▲ For the stuffing, melt the butter or margarine in a small saucepan. Add the onion and cook over medium heat until softened, about 5 minutes. Stir in the spinach and cook, stirring constantly, until the spinach wilts and renders its liquid.

~ **VARIATION** ~

Instead of sole, other lean fish fillets may be used, such as flounder, whitefish, perch, or orange roughy.

3 Add the pine nuts, raisins, bread crumbs, cinnamon, and a little salt and pepper. Raise the heat and cook until most of the liquid has evaporated, stirring constantly. Remove from the heat.

4 ▲ Sprinkle the sole fillets with salt and pepper. Place a spoonful of the spinach stuffing at one end of each fillet. Roll up and secure with a wooden toothpick, if necessary.

5 ▲ Place the sole rolls in the prepared baking dish. Put a small piece of butter or margarine on each roll. Pour the wine over the fish. Cover the baking dish with foil and bake until the fish flakes easily when tested with a fork, about 15 minutes.

6 Serve on warmed plates with a little of the cooking juices spooned over the fish.

Salmon Steaks with Lime Butter

SERVES 4

4 salmon steaks (about 1½ pounds)

salt and pepper

FOR THE LIME BUTTER

4 tablespoons butter or margarine, at
   room temperature

1 tablespoon chopped fresh coriander
   (cilantro), or 1 teaspoon dried
   coriander

1 teaspoon finely grated lime rind

1 tablespoon fresh lime juice

1 For the lime butter, combine the
butter or margarine, coriander, and
lime rind and juice in a bowl. Mix
well with a fork.

2 ▲ Transfer the lime butter to a
piece of wax paper and shape into a
log. Roll in the paper until smooth
and round. Refrigerate until firm,
about 1 hour.

3 Preheat the broiler.

4 ▼ Sprinkle the salmon steaks with
salt and pepper. Arrange them on the
rack in the broiler pan. Broil about 3
inches from the heat, 5 minutes on
each side.

5 Unwrap the lime butter and cut
into 4 pieces. Top each salmon steak
with a pat of lime butter and serve.

Citrus Fish Fillets

SERVES 6

1–2 tablespoons butter or margarine,
   melted

2 pounds sole fillets

salt and pepper

1 teaspoon grated lemon rind

1 teaspoon grated orange rind

2 tablespoons fresh orange juice

⅓ cup whipping cream

1 tablespoon chopped fresh basil

fresh basil sprigs, for garnishing

1 Preheat the oven to 350°F.
Generously grease a large baking dish
with the melted butter or margarine.

> ~ **VARIATION** ~
>
> Use an equal amount of grapefruit
> rind and juice to replace the
> lemon and orange.

2 ▲ Lay the fish fillets skin-side
down in the baking dish, in one layer.
Sprinkle with salt and pepper.

3 ▲ In a small bowl, combine the
lemon and orange rinds and orange
juice. Pour the mixture over the fish.

4 Bake until the fish flakes easily
when tested with a fork, 15–20
minutes. Transfer the fish to a warmed
serving platter.

5 ▲ Strain the juices from the
baking dish into a small saucepan. Stir
in the cream and chopped basil. Boil
until thickened, about 5 minutes.

6 Spoon the citrus cream over the
fish fillets. Garnish with basil sprigs
and serve.

Salmon Steaks with Lime Butter (top), Citrus Fish Fillets

Sweet and Spicy Salmon Fillets

SERVES 6

2 pounds salmon fillet, cut in 6 pieces

½ cup honey

¼ cup soy sauce

juice of 1 lime

1 tablespoon sesame oil

¼ teaspoon hot red pepper flakes

¼ teaspoon crushed black peppercorns

~ COOK'S TIP ~

The acid in the citrus juice begins to "cook" the fish, so broiling on one side only is sufficient.

1 Place the salmon pieces skin-side down in a large baking dish, in one layer.

2 ▲ In a bowl, combine the honey, soy sauce, lime juice, sesame oil, pepper flakes, and peppercorns.

3 ▲ Pour the mixture over the fish. Cover and let marinate 30 minutes.

4 Preheat the broiler. Remove the fish from the marinade and arrange on the rack in the broiler pan, skin-side down. Broil about 3 inches from the heat until the fish flakes easily when tested with a fork, 6–8 minutes.

Peppercorn-Crusted Cod Steaks

SERVES 4

1 teaspoon each pink, white, and green peppercorns

3 tablespoons butter or margarine

4 cod steaks, each 1-inch thick (about 1 pound)

salt

½ cup fish stock or bottled clam juice

½ cup whipping cream

¼ cup chopped fresh chives

1 ▼ Wrap the peppercorns in a dish towel or heavy plastic bag and crush with a rolling pin.

2 Melt the butter or margarine in a large frying pan. Remove from the heat. Brush the cod steaks with some of the butter or margarine.

3 ▲ Press the crushed peppercorns onto both sides of the cod steaks. Season with salt.

4 Heat the frying pan. Add the cod steaks and cook over medium-low heat until the fish flakes easily when tested with a fork, about 4 minutes on each side. Transfer the steaks to a warmed serving platter.

5 ▲ Add the stock or clam juice and cream to the frying pan and bring to a boil, stirring well. Boil until reduced by half, about 5 minutes. Remove from the heat and stir in the chives.

6 Pour the sauce over the fish and serve immediately.

~ VARIATION ~

In place of cod, use monkfish, cut into steaks or thick fillets. The flavor is similar to lobster.

Sweet and Spicy Salmon Fillets (top), Peppercorn-Crusted Cod Steaks

Red Snapper Veracruz

SERVES 4

3 tablespoons flour

salt and pepper

1½ pounds red snapper fillets or other firm white-fish fillets

1 tablespoon butter or margarine

2 tablespoons olive oil

1 onion, sliced

2 garlic cloves, chopped

¼ teaspoon ground cumin

1½ cups peeled, seeded, and chopped fresh tomatoes or canned crushed tomatoes

½ cup fresh orange juice

orange wedges, for garnishing

1 ▼ Put the flour on a plate and season with salt and pepper. Coat the fish fillets lightly with the seasoned flour, shaking off any excess.

2 Heat the butter or margarine and half the oil in a large skillet. Add the fish fillets to the skillet and cook until golden brown and the flesh flakes easily when tested with a fork, about 3 minutes on each side.

3 ▲ When the fish is cooked, transfer to a heated serving platter. Cover with foil and keep warm while making the sauce.

4 ▲ Heat the remaining oil in the skillet. Add the onion and garlic and cook until softened, about 5 minutes.

5 ▲ Stir in the cumin, tomatoes, and orange juice. Bring to a boil and cook until thickened, about 10 minutes, stirring frequently.

6 Garnish the fish with orange wedges. Pass the sauce separately.

Baked Stuffed Trout

SERVES 4

2 tablespoons butter or margarine

1 onion, chopped

1 celery stalk, diced

1 cup fresh bread cubes

1 tablespoon fresh thyme leaves or 1
   teaspoon dried thyme

salt and pepper

4 trout, dressed (about ½ pound each)

8 bacon slices

celery leaves or parsley, for garnishing

1 Preheat the oven to 450°F.

2 ▲ Melt the butter or margarine in
a frying pan. Add the onion and
celery and cook until softened, about
5 minutes. Remove the pan from the
heat. Add the bread cubes, thyme,
and season with salt and pepper to
taste. Stir to mix well.

3 ▲ Season the cavity of each trout
with salt and pepper.

4 ▲ Stuff each trout with the bread
mixture, dividing it evenly among the
fish. If necessary, secure the openings
with wooden toothpicks.

5 ▼ Wrap 2 bacon slices around
each stuffed trout. Arrange in a
baking dish, in one layer.

6 Bake until the fish flakes easily
when tested with a fork and the bacon
is crisp, 35–40 minutes. Serve
garnished with celery leaves or sprigs
of parsley.

Seafood and Vegetable Stir-Fry

SERVES 4

1 pound rice vermicelli

2 tablespoons oil drained from sun-dried tomatoes

½ cup sun-dried tomatoes packed in oil, drained and sliced

½ cup scallions, cut diagonally in ½-inch pieces

2 large carrots, cut in thin sticks

1 zucchini, cut in thin sticks

½ pound raw shrimp, peeled and deveined

½ pound sea scallops

1-inch piece of fresh gingerroot, peeled and finely grated

3 tablespoons fresh lemon juice

3 tablespoons chopped fresh basil or 1 teaspoon dried basil

salt and pepper

1 ▲ Bring a large saucepan of water to a boil. Add the rice vermicelli and cook until tender (check package directions for timing). Drain, rinse with boiling water, and drain again thoroughly. Keep warm.

2 ▲ Heat the oil in a wok over high heat. Add the tomatoes, scallions, and carrots and stir-fry 5 minutes.

3 ▲ Add the zucchini, shrimp, scallops, and gingerroot. Stir-fry 3 minutes.

4 ▲ Add the lemon juice, basil, and salt and pepper to taste and stir well. Stir-fry until the shrimp are all pink, about 2 more minutes.

5 Serve on the rice vermicelli.

Seafood Stew

SERVES 6

3 tablespoons olive oil

2 large onions, chopped

1 small green bell pepper, seeded and sliced

3 carrots, chopped

3 garlic cloves, minced

2 tablespoons tomato paste

2 16-ounce cans crushed tomatoes

¼ cup chopped fresh parsley

1 teaspoon fresh thyme leaves or ¼ teaspoon dried thyme

1 tablespoon chopped fresh basil or 1 teaspoon dried basil

½ cup dry white wine

1 pound raw shrimp, peeled and deveined

3 pounds mussels or clams (in shells), or a mixture of both, thoroughly cleaned

2 pounds halibut fillet, cut in 2- to 3-inch pieces

1½ cups fish stock or water

salt and pepper

extra chopped fresh herbs, for garnishing

1 ▲ Heat the oil in a flameproof casserole. Add the onions, green bell pepper, carrots, and garlic and cook until tender, about 5 minutes.

2 Add the tomato paste, canned tomatoes, herbs, and wine and stir well to combine. Bring to a boil and simmer 20 minutes.

3 ▲ Add the shrimp, mussels, clams, halibut pieces and stock. Season with salt and pepper.

4 ▲ Bring back to a boil, then reduce the heat and simmer until the shrimp turn pink, the pieces of fish will flake easily, and the mussels and clams open, about 5 minutes.

5 Serve in large soup plates, garnished with chopped herbs.

New England Clambake with Lobster

SERVES 6

fresh seaweed

salt

6 1-pound lobsters

2 pounds pickling onions, peeled

2 pounds small red potatoes

3 dozen littleneck or cherrystone clams

6 ears of corn, husks and silk removed

1 cup (2 sticks) butter or margarine

3 tablespoons chopped fresh chives

1 Put a layer of seaweed in the bottom of a deep kettle containing 1 inch of salted water. Put the lobsters on top and cover with more seaweed.

2 Add the onions and potatoes. Cover the kettle and bring the water to a boil.

3 ▲ After 10 minutes, add the clams and the ears of corn. Cover again and cook until the clams have opened, the lobster shells are red, and the potatoes are tender, 15–20 minutes longer.

4 ▲ Meanwhile, in a small saucepan melt the butter or margarine and stir in the chives.

5 Discard the seaweed. Serve the lobsters and clams with the vegetables, accompanied by the chive butter.

Scallop Kabobs

SERVES 4

16 sea scallops

½ teaspoon ground ginger

1 8-ounce can pineapple chunks in juice, drained and juice reserved

1 small fresh red chili pepper, seeded and chopped

grated rind and juice of 1 lime

16 snow peas

16 cherry tomatoes

8 baby zucchini, halved

1 Put the scallops in a bowl. Add the ginger, the juice from the pineapple, the chili pepper, and lime rind and juice and stir well. Cover and let marinate at room temperature about 20 minutes, or 2 hours in the refrigerator.

2 Preheat the broiler.

3 ▲ Drain the scallops, reserving their marinade. Wrap a snow pea around a scallop and thread onto 1 of 4 skewers. Thread on a cherry tomato, a piece of zucchini, and a piece of pineapple, followed by another snow pea-wrapped scallop. Repeat until all the ingredients have been used.

4 ▲ Lay the kabobs in the broiler pan and brush with the reserved marinade.

5 Broil about 3 inches from the heat, brushing frequently with the marinade and turning occasionally, until the scallops are opaque, 4–5 minutes.

6 Serve immediately, on a bed of cooked rice, if wished.

New England Clambake with Lobster (top), Scallop Kabobs

MEAT & POULTRY

~

For most people, meat and poultry are the heart of a good meal, so new and interesting recipes for beef, lamb, pork, chicken, and turkey are always welcome. Here are lots of good ideas, from snacks to barbecue fare, and stews to roasts.

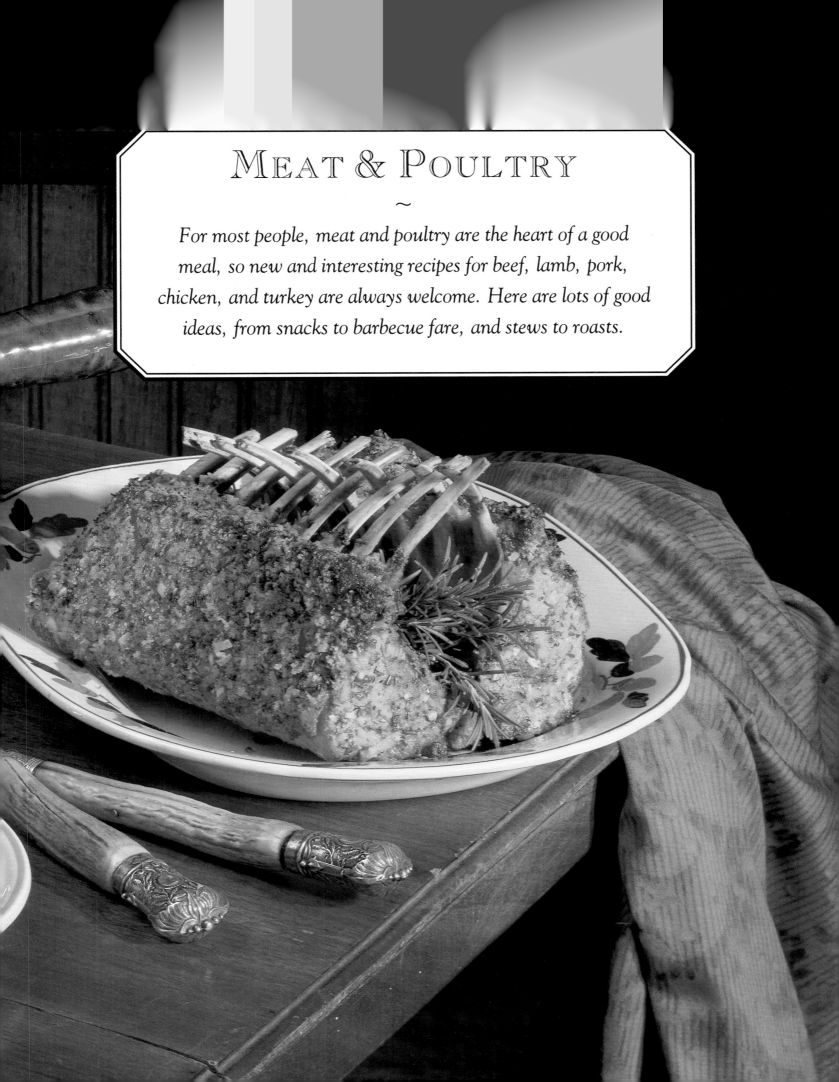

Old-Fashioned Beef Stew

SERVES 6

3 tablespoons corn oil

1 large onion, sliced

2 carrots, chopped

1 celery stalk, chopped

2 tablespoons flour

3 tablespoons paprika

2 pounds beef chuck steak, cubed

2 tablespoons tomato paste

1 cup red wine

2 cups beef stock

1 sprig of fresh thyme or 1 teaspoon
dried thyme

1 bay leaf

salt and pepper

3 medium potatoes, cut into 1½-inch
pieces

1 cup button mushrooms, quartered

1 Preheat the oven to 375°F.

2 ▼ Heat half the oil in a large
flameproof casserole. Add the onion,
carrots, and celery and cook until
softened, about 5 minutes. Remove
the vegetables with a slotted spoon
and set aside.

3 ▲ Combine the flour and paprika
in a plastic bag. Add the beef cubes
and shake to coat them with the
seasoned flour.

4 Heat the remaining oil in the
casserole. Add the beef cubes and
brown well on all sides, about 10
minutes.

5 Return the vegetables to the
casserole. Stir in the tomato paste, red
wine, stock, thyme, bay leaf, and a
little salt and pepper. Bring to a boil.

6 ▲ Stir in the potatoes. Cover the
casserole and transfer it to the oven.
Cook 1 hour.

7 Stir in the mushrooms and
continue cooking until the beef is very
tender, about 30 minutes longer.
Discard the bay leaf before serving.

Steak, Bell Pepper, and Corn Stir-Fry

SERVES 4

2–3 teaspoons chili powder

1 teaspoon ground cumin

½ teaspoon dried oregano

salt and pepper

1 pound beef top round steak, cut into thin strips

2 tablespoons corn oil

5 scallions, cut on the diagonal into 1-inch lengths

1 small green bell pepper, cored and thinly sliced

1 small red bell pepper, cored and thinly sliced

1 small yellow bell pepper, cored and thinly sliced

¼ pound baby corn, halved lengthwise, or 1 cup corn kernels

4 garlic cloves, minced

2 tablespoons fresh lime juice

2 tablespoons chopped fresh coriander leaves (cilantro)

1 ▼ In a medium bowl, combine the spices, oregano, and a little salt and pepper. Rub the mixture into the steak strips.

2 Heat half the oil in a wok or large frying pan over high heat. Add the steak strips and stir-fry until well browned on all sides, 3–4 minutes. Remove the steak from the wok with a slotted spoon and keep hot.

3 ▲ Heat the remaining oil in the wok and add the scallions, bell peppers, corn, and garlic. Stir-fry until the vegetables are crisp-tender, about 3 minutes.

4 ▼ Return the steak to the wok and toss briefly to mix with the vegetables and heat it through. Stir in the lime juice and coriander and serve.

Guacamole Cheeseburgers

SERVES 6

2 pounds ground chuck

salt and pepper

6 slices of Swiss cheese

6 hamburger buns with sesame seeds, split and toasted

2 large tomatoes, sliced

FOR THE GUACAMOLE

1 large ripe avocado

1 scallion, chopped

2 teaspoons fresh lemon juice

1 teaspoon chili powder

2 tablespoons chopped fresh tomato

1 To make the guacamole, peel the avocado, discard the pit, and mash the flesh with a fork. Stir in the scallion, lemon juice, chili powder, and chopped tomato. Set aside.

2 Preheat the broiler.

3 ▼ Handling the beef as little as possible, divide it into 6 equal portions. Shape each portion into a ¾-inch-thick patty and season.

4 Arrange the patties on the rack in the broiler pan. Broil about 3 inches from the heat, 5 minutes on each side for medium-rare, 8 minutes on each side for well-done.

5 ▲ Top each hamburger with a slice of cheese and broil until melted, about 30 seconds.

6 Set a hamburger in each toasted bun. Top with a slice of tomato and a spoonful of guacamole and serve.

Chili con Carne

SERVES 8

3 tablespoons corn oil

1 large onion, chopped

2 pounds ground chuck

4 garlic cloves, minced

1 tablespoon light brown sugar

2-3 tablespoons chili powder

1 teaspoon ground cumin

1 teaspoon salt

1 teaspoon pepper

½ cup tomato paste

1 cup beer

2 cups tomato sauce

2 cups cooked or canned red kidney beans, rinsed and drained

FOR SERVING

1 pound spaghetti, broken in half

1 cup sour cream

2 cups shredded Monterey jack or cheddar cheese

1 Heat the oil in a deep saucepan and cook the onion until softened, about 5 minutes. Add the beef and cook until browned, breaking up the meat with the side of a spoon.

2 ▼ Stir in the garlic, brown sugar, chili powder, cumin, salt, and pepper. Add the tomato paste, beer, and tomato sauce and stir to mix. Bring to a boil. Reduce the heat, cover, and simmer 50 minutes.

3 ▲ Stir in the kidney beans and simmer 5 minutes longer, uncovered.

4 Meanwhile, cook the spaghetti in a large pot of boiling salted water until just tender (check package directions for cooking time). Drain.

5 To serve, put the spaghetti into a warmed bowl. Ladle the chili over the spaghetti and top with some of the sour cream and shredded cheese. Serve the remaining sour cream and cheese separately.

Guacamole Cheeseburgers (top), Chili con Carne

Pork with Mustard-Peppercorn Sauce

SERVES 4

2 pork tenderloins, about ¾ pound each

2 tablespoons butter or margarine

1 tablespoon olive oil

1 tablespoon red wine vinegar

1 tablespoon whole-grain mustard

3 tablespoons whipping cream

1 tablespoon green peppercorns in
   brine, drained

pinch salt

1 Cut the pork tenderloins across
into 1-inch-thick slices.

2 ▼ Heat the butter or margarine
and oil in a frying pan. Add the slices
of pork and fry until browned and
cooked through, 5–8 minutes on each
side. Transfer the pork to a warmed
serving plate and keep hot.

3 ▼ Add the vinegar and mustard to
the pan and cook 1 minute, stirring
with a wooden spoon to loosen any
particles attached to the bottom.

4 Stir in the cream, peppercorns, and
salt. Boil 1 minute. Pour the sauce
over the pork and serve immediately.

Pork Chop, Potato, and Apple Scallop

SERVES 6

2 cups apple juice

½ pound baking potatoes, peeled and
   cut into ½-inch slices

½ pound sweet potatoes, peeled and cut
   into ½-inch slices

1 pound apples, peeled, cored, and cut
   into ½-inch slices

salt and pepper

6 tablespoons flour

6 pork chops, cut 1-inch thick, trimmed
   of excess fat

4 tablespoons butter or margarine

3 tablespoons corn oil

6 fresh sage leaves

1 Preheat the oven to 350°F. Grease
a 13- × 9-inch baking dish.

2 In a small saucepan, bring the apple
juice to a boil.

3 ▼ Arrange a row of baking-potato
slices at a short end of the prepared
dish. Arrange a row of sweet-potato
slices next to the first row, slightly
overlapping it, and then a row of
apple slices. Repeat the alternating
overlapping rows to fill the dish.
Sprinkle with salt and pepper.

4 Pour the apple juice over the potato
and apple slices. Cover the dish with
foil and bake 40 minutes.

5 ▲ Meanwhile, season the flour
with salt and pepper. Coat the chops
with the seasoned flour, shaking off
any excess. Melt the butter or
margarine with the oil in a frying pan.
Fry the chops until well browned,
about 5 minutes on each side.

6 Uncover the baking dish. Arrange
the chops on top of the potatoes and
apples. Put a sage leaf on each chop.

7 Return to the oven, uncovered,
and cook until the potatoes and pork
chops are tender and most of the
liquid is absorbed, about 1 hour.

Pork with Mustard-Peppercorn Sauce (top), Pork Chop, Potato, and Apple Scallop

Glazed Lamb Kabobs

SERVES 4

1 pound boned leg of lamb, cut into 1-inch cubes
3 medium zucchini, cut into ½-inch slices
¼ cup mint jelly
2 tablespoons fresh lemon juice
2 tablespoons olive oil
1 tablespoon chopped fresh mint

~ **VARIATION** ~

Substitute an equal quantity of orange marmalade for the mint jelly. Instead of fresh mint, use 2 teaspoons of grated orange rind.

1   Preheat the broiler.

2   Thread the cubes of lamb and slices of zucchini alternately onto metal or wooden skewers.

3 ▲ Combine the mint jelly, lemon juice, olive oil, and chopped mint in a small saucepan. Stir over low heat until the jelly melts.

4 ▼ Brush the lamb and zucchini with the mint glaze. Lay them on the rack in the broiler pan.

5   Cook under the broiler, about 3 inches from the heat, until browned and cooked to taste, 10–12 minutes, turning the skewers frequently. Serve on a bed of rice, if wished.

Lamb Burgers with Cucumber-Mint Relish

SERVES 4

1½ pounds ground lamb
1 medium onion, finely chopped
1 tablespoon paprika
2 tablespoons chopped fresh parsley
2 tablespoons chopped fresh mint or 1 tablespoon dried mint
salt and pepper
4 hamburger buns with sesame seeds, split open

FOR THE RELISH

2 medium hothouse cucumbers, thinly sliced
1 small red onion, thinly sliced
3 tablespoons fresh lime juice
2 teaspoons vegetable oil
½ cup chopped fresh mint or 2 tablespoons dried mint
2 scallions, finely chopped

1   To make the relish, combine the cucumbers, red onion, lime juice, oil, mint, and scallions in a non-metallic bowl. Cover the mixture and refrigerate at least 2 hours.

2 ▲ In a bowl, combine the lamb, onion, paprika, parsley, mint, and a little salt and pepper. Mix thoroughly.

3   Preheat the broiler.

4 ▲ Divide the lamb mixture into 4 equal portions and shape each into a 1-inch-thick patty.

5   Broil the burgers, about 3 inches from the heat, allowing 5 minutes on each side for medium and 8 minutes on each side for well-done. At the same time, toast the cut surfaces of the buns briefly under the broiler.

6   Serve the lamb burgers in the buns, with the cucumber-mint relish.

Glazed Lamb Kabobs (top), Lamb Burgers with Cucumber-Mint Relish

Sesame Lamb Chops

SERVES 4

8 lamb rib chops

salt and pepper

1 egg

1 teaspoon Dijon-style mustard

3 tablespoons fine dry bread crumbs

3 tablespoons sesame seeds

2 tablespoons flour

2 tablespoons butter or margarine

1 tablespoon oil

1 ▼ If necessary, trim any excess fat from the chops. With a small knife, scrape all the meat and fat off the top 2 inches of the bone in each chop. Sprinkle the chops generously with salt and pepper.

2 ▲ In a bowl, beat the egg and mustard together. Pour into a shallow dish. In another dish, mix the bread crumbs and sesame seeds. Place the flour in a third dish.

3 ▲ Dredge each chop in flour, shaking off any excess. Dip in the egg and mustard mixture and then coat with the bread crumb mixture, pressing it on the meat to get an even coating. Refrigerate 15 minutes.

4 ▲ Heat the butter or margarine and oil in a frying pan. Add the chops and fry over medium heat until crisp and golden and cooked to taste, 4–5 minutes on each side, turning gently with tongs.

Roast Rack of Lamb

SERVES 4

2 racks of lamb, each with 8 chops, ends
  of bones scraped clean

¼ cup Dijon-style mustard

1½ tablespoons fresh rosemary or 1
  tablespoon dried rosemary

salt and pepper

½ cup fine dry bread crumbs

¼ cup chopped fresh parsley

4 garlic cloves, minced

¼ cup olive oil

½ cup butter or margarine

1 cup chicken stock

1 Preheat the oven to 425°F.

2 ▲ Brush the meaty side of the
racks with the mustard. Sprinkle with
the rosemary, salt, and pepper.

3 ▲ In a bowl, mix the bread crumbs
with the parsley, garlic, and half of
the olive oil. Press this mixture evenly
over the mustard on the racks of lamb.
Wrap the scraped bone ends with foil.
Put the racks in a roasting pan.

4 In a small saucepan, melt half the
butter or margarine. Stir in the
remaining olive oil. Drizzle this
mixture over the crumb coating.

5 Roast the racks of lamb, allowing
40 minutes for medium-rare meat and
50 minutes for medium.

6 Transfer the racks to a warmed
serving platter, arranging them so the
scraped ends of the bones are
interlocked. Cover loosely with foil
and set aside.

7 Pour the stock into the roasting pan
and bring to a boil, scraping the
bottom of the pan with a wooden
spoon to mix in all the cooking juices.
Remove from the heat and swirl in the
remaining butter or margarine. Pour
the gravy into a warmed sauceboat.

8 To serve, carve each rack by
cutting down between the chop
bones, or cut down after every 2 bones
for double chops.

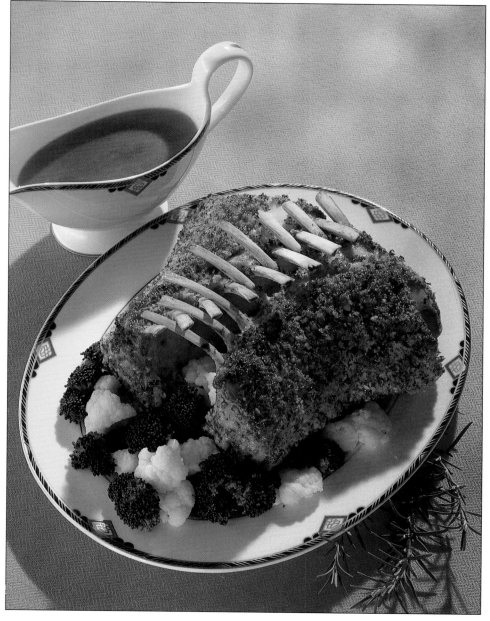

Chicken Breasts with Prunes and Almonds

2 tablespoons butter or margarine

1 tablespoon corn oil

2½ pounds chicken breast halves

3 cups chicken stock

⅔ cup raisins

1 tablespoon fresh thyme leaves or 1 teaspoon dried thyme

3 fresh sage leaves, chopped

¼ cup chopped fresh parsley

1 tablespoon chopped fresh marjoram or 1 teaspoon dried marjoram

1 cup fresh bread crumbs

½ cup ground almonds

12 prunes, pitted

4–6 whole cloves

½ teaspoon ground mace

pinch of saffron threads, crumbled

salt and pepper

⅓ cup sliced almonds, toasted

1 ▼ Melt the butter or margarine with the oil in a frying pan. Add the chicken and brown 10 minutes, turning once. Transfer the chicken pieces to a large pot.

~ **COOK'S TIP** ~

For ground almonds, chop whole or slivered almonds in a food processor until powdery.

2 ▲ Pour the stock into the pot and bring to a boil. Add all the remaining ingredients, except the toasted almonds, and stir well to mix. Simmer 45 minutes.

3 ▲ With tongs, remove the chicken from the pot and let cool. Bring the cooking liquid back to a boil and boil until well reduced, about 10 minutes, stirring frequently.

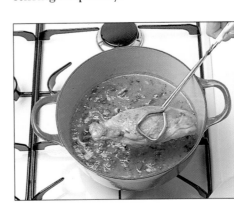

4 ▲ Remove the bones from the chicken and return the meat to the sauce. Heat through. Serve sprinkled with the toasted almonds.

Southern Fried Chicken

SERVES 4

½ cup buttermilk

1 3-pound chicken, cut into pieces

corn oil for frying

½ cup flour

1 tablespoon paprika

¼ teaspoon pepper

1 tablespoon water

1 ▼ Pour the buttermilk into a large bowl and add the chicken pieces. Stir to coat, then set aside for 5 minutes.

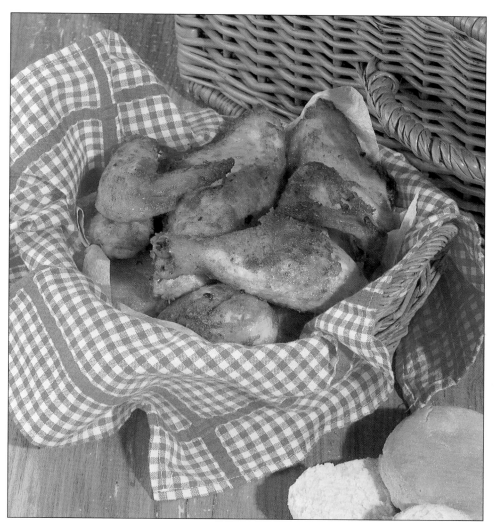

2 Heat a ¼-inch layer of oil in a large frying pan over medium-high heat. Do not let oil overheat.

3 ▲ In a bowl or plastic bag, combine the flour, paprika, and pepper. One by one, lift the chicken pieces out of the buttermilk and dip into the flour to coat all over, shaking off any excess.

4 ▼ Add the chicken pieces to the hot oil and fry until lightly browned, about 10 minutes, turning over halfway through cooking time.

5 ▲ Reduce the heat to low and add the water to the frying pan. Cover and cook 30 minutes, turning the pieces over at 10-minute intervals. Uncover the pan and continue cooking until the chicken is very tender and the coating is crisp, about 15 minutes, turning every 5 minutes. Serve hot.

Cornish Game Hens with Cranberry Sauce

SERVES 4

4 Cornish game hens, with giblets, each about 1 pound

3 tablespoons butter or margarine

salt and pepper

1 onion, quartered

¼ cup port wine

⅔ cup chicken stock

2 tablespoons honey

1½ cups fresh cranberries

~ **VARIATION** ~

For extra zest, add 2 tablespoons of finely grated orange rind to the sauce with the cranberries.

1 Preheat the oven to 450°F.

2 ▼ Smear the hens on all sides with 2 tablespoons of the butter or margarine. Arrange them, on their sides, in a roasting pan in which they will fit comfortably. Sprinkle them with salt and pepper. Add the onion quarters to the pan. Chop the gizzards and livers and arrange them around the hens.

3 ▲ Roast 20 minutes, basting often with the melted fat in the pan. Turn the hens onto their other sides and roast 20 minutes longer, basting often. Turn the hens breast up and continue roasting until they are cooked through, about 15 minutes. Transfer the hens to a warmed serving dish. Cover with foil and set aside.

4 Skim any fat off the juices in the roasting pan. Put the pan on top of the stove and bring the juices to a boil. Add the port wine and bring back to a boil, stirring well to dislodge any particles attached to the bottom of the pan.

5 ▲ Strain the sauce into a small saucepan. Add the stock, bring to a boil, and boil until reduced by half. Stir in the honey and cranberries. Simmer until the cranberries pop, about 3 minutes.

6 Remove the pan from the heat and swirl in the remaining butter or margarine. Season to taste with salt and pepper. Pour the sauce into a sauceboat and serve with the hens.

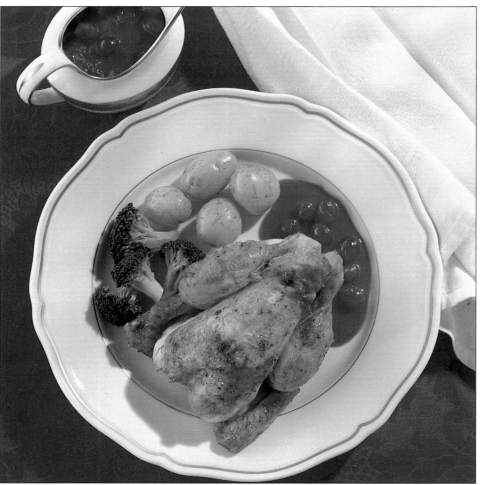

Barbecue Chicken

SERVES 4

3 tablespoons corn oil
1 large onion, chopped
¾ cup catsup
¾ cup water
2½ tablespoons fresh lemon juice
1½ tablespoons prepared horseradish
1 tablespoon light brown sugar
1 tablespoon spicy brown mustard
3 pounds chicken pieces

1 Preheat the oven to 350°F.

2 ▲ Heat 1 tablespoon of the oil in a saucepan. Add the onion and cook until softened, about 5 minutes. Stir in the catsup, water, lemon juice, horseradish, brown sugar, and mustard and bring to a boil. Reduce the heat and simmer the sauce 10 minutes, stirring occasionally.

3 ▲ Heat the remaining oil in a heavy frying pan. Add the chicken pieces and brown on all sides. Drain the chicken pieces on paper towels.

4 ▼ Transfer the chicken pieces to a 11- × 9-inch baking dish and pour the sauce over the top.

5 ▲ Bake until the chicken is cooked and tender, about 1¼ hours, basting occasionally. Alternatively, grill over medium coals for 40–50 minutes, turning once and brushing frequently with the sauce.

Honey Roast Chicken

SERVES 4

1 3½-pound chicken
2 tablespoons clear honey
1 tablespoon brandy
1½ tablespoons flour
⅔ cup chicken stock
FOR THE STUFFING
2 shallots, chopped
4 bacon slices, chopped
½ cup button mushrooms, quartered
1 tablespoon butter or margarine
2 thick slices of white bread, diced
1 tablespoon chopped fresh parsley
salt and pepper

1 ▼ For the stuffing, gently fry the shallots, bacon, and mushrooms in a frying pan for 5 minutes. With a slotted spoon, transfer them to a bowl.

2 Pour off all but 2 tablespoons of bacon fat from the pan. Add the butter or margarine to the pan and fry the bread until golden brown. Add the bread to the bacon mixture. Stir in the parsley and salt and pepper to taste. Let cool.

3 Preheat the oven to 350°F.

4 ▲ Pack the stuffing into the body cavity of the chicken. Truss it with string, or secure with poultry pins, to keep it in a neat shape.

5 ▲ Transfer the chicken to a roasting pan which just holds it comfortably.

6 ▲ Mix the honey with the brandy. Brush half of the mixture over the chicken. Roast until the chicken is thoroughly cooked, about 1 hour 20 minutes. Baste the chicken frequently with the remaining honey mixture during roasting.

7 ▲ Transfer the chicken to a warmed serving platter. Cover with foil and set aside.

8 ▲ Strain the cooking juices into a degreasing pitcher. Set aside to let the fat rise to the surface.

9 ▲ Stir the flour into the sediments in the roasting pan. Add the lean part of the juices and the stock. Boil rapidly until the gravy has thickened, stirring constantly.

10 Pour the gravy into a warmed sauceboat and serve with the chicken.

Chicken Thighs Wrapped in Bacon

SERVES 4

16 bacon slices

8 chicken thighs, skin removed

FOR THE MARINADE

finely grated rind and juice of 1 orange

finely grated rind and juice of 1 lime

5 garlic cloves, minced

1 tablespoon chili powder

1 tablespoon paprika

1 teaspoon ground cumin

½ teaspoon dried oregano

1 tablespoon olive oil

1 For the marinade, combine the citrus rind and juice, garlic, chili powder, paprika, cumin, oregano, and olive oil in a bowl.

2 ▲ Wrap 2 slices of bacon around each chicken thigh in a cross shape. Secure with wooden toothpicks. Arrange the wrapped chicken thighs in a baking dish.

3 Pour the marinade over the chicken, cover, and let marinate 1 hour at room temperature or several hours in the refrigerator.

4 Preheat the oven to 375°F.

5 ▼ Put the baking dish in the oven and bake until the chicken is cooked through and the bacon is crisp, about 40 minutes for small thighs and 1 hour for large thighs. Skim excess fat from the sauce before serving. Rice is a good accompaniment because there is plenty of sauce.

Deviled Chicken Drumsticks

SERVES 4

2 tablespoons corn oil

8 chicken drumsticks, about 3 pounds

1 medium onion, chopped

½ cup water

¼ cup Dijon-style mustard

1 tablespoon prepared horseradish

1 tablespoon Worcestershire sauce

1 teaspoon light brown sugar

¼ teaspoon salt

parsley sprigs, for garnishing

1 Heat the oil in a frying pan. Add the chicken drumsticks and brown them on all sides. With a spatula or tongs, remove the drumsticks from the pan and drain on paper towels.

2 ▲ Add the onion to the hot oil and cook until softened, about 5 minutes. Return the chicken to the pan. Stir in the water, mustard, horseradish, Worcestershire sauce, brown sugar, and salt. Bring to a boil.

3 Reduce the heat to low. Cover the pan and simmer until the chicken is very tender, about 45 minutes, stirring occasionally.

4 ▼ Transfer the drumsticks to a warmed serving dish. Skim any fat off the cooking juices. Pour the juices over the chicken. Garnish with parsley and serve.

Chicken Thighs Wrapped in Bacon (top), Deviled Chicken Drumsticks

Turkey Kiev

SERVES 4

4 turkey cutlets (boneless slices of breast), about 6 ounces each

salt and pepper

½ cup butter or margarine, chilled

1 teaspoon grated orange rind

2 tablespoons chopped fresh chives

flour, for dredging

3 eggs, beaten

1 cup fine dry bread crumbs

corn oil, for frying

orange wedges and parsley, for garnishing

1 ▼ Place each cutlet between 2 sheets of wax paper. With the flat side of a meat pounder, pound until about ¼-inch thick, being careful not to split the meat. Remove the wax paper. Sprinkle the cutlets with salt and pepper.

2 ▲ Cut the butter or margarine into 4 finger-shaped pieces. Place a piece crosswise in the middle of a cutlet. Sprinkle with a little orange rind and chives.

3 ▲ Fold in the 2 long sides of the cutlet, then roll up from a short end. Secure with wooden toothpicks. Repeat with the remaining cutlets.

4 Dredge each roll lightly with flour, shaking off any excess. Dip in the beaten eggs, then roll in the bread crumbs to coat evenly on all sides. Refrigerate 1 hour to set the breaded coating.

5 Pour enough oil into a frying pan to make a ½-inch layer and heat. Add the breaded turkey rolls to the hot oil and fry until crisp and golden on all sides, 15–20 minutes, turning gently with tongs.

6 Remove the toothpicks before serving. Garnish with orange wedges and parsley.

Turkey Scaloppine with Lemon and Sage

4 turkey cutlets (boneless slices of breast), about 6 ounces each

salt and pepper

1 tablespoon freshly grated lemon rind

1 tablespoon chopped fresh sage or 1 teaspoon dried sage

¼ cup fresh lemon juice

6 tablespoons vegetable oil

1 cup fine dry bread crumbs

fresh sage leaves, for garnishing

lemon slices, for garnishing

1 Place each cutlet between 2 sheets of wax paper. With the flat side of a meat pounder, pound until about ¼-inch thick, being careful not to split the meat. Remove the wax paper. Sprinkle the cutlets with salt and pepper.

2 ▲ In a small bowl, combine the lemon rind, sage, lemon juice, and 2 tablespoons of the oil. Stir well to mix.

~ **VARIATION** ~

For a delicious alternative, substitute fresh tarragon leaves for the sage.

3 ▼ Arrange the turkey cutlets, in one layer, in 1 or 2 shallow baking dishes. Divide the lemon mixture evenly between the dishes and rub well into the turkey. Let marinate 20 minutes.

4 ▲ Heat the remaining oil in a frying pan. Dredge the turkey scaloppine in the bread crumbs, shaking off the excess. Fry in the hot oil until golden brown, about 2 minutes on each side. Serve garnished with sage leaves and lemon slices.

SALADS, VEGETABLES, EGGS & CHEESE

~

Here's a bright selection of tasty vegetable main dishes and accompaniments, colorful salads, and economical and quickly-made egg and cheese dishes, for lunch or supper.

Avocado, Grapefruit, and Canteloupe Salad

SERVES 6

1 pink grapefruit

1 white or yellow grapefruit

1 cantaloupe

2 large, ripe but firm avocados

2 tablespoons fresh lemon juice

2 tablespoons vegetable oil

1 tablespoon clear honey

¼ cup chopped fresh mint

salt and pepper

fresh mint leaves, for garnishing

1 ▲ Peel the grapefruit. Cut out the sections, leaving the membranes. Put the sections in a bowl.

2 Cut the melon in half. Remove the seeds and discard them. With a melon baller, scoop out balls from the melon flesh. Add the melon balls to the grapefruit sections. Chill the fruit at least 30 minutes.

3 ▲ Cut the avocados in half and discard the pits. Cut each half in two. Peel the skin, then cut the flesh into small pieces.

4 ▲ Toss the avocado pieces in the lemon juice. Using a slotted spoon, transfer the avocado to the grapefruit mixture.

5 ▲ For the dressing, whisk the oil into the reserved lemon juice. Stir in the honey, chopped mint, and salt and pepper to taste.

6 Pour the dressing over the fruit mixture and toss gently. Garnish with mint leaves and serve immediately.

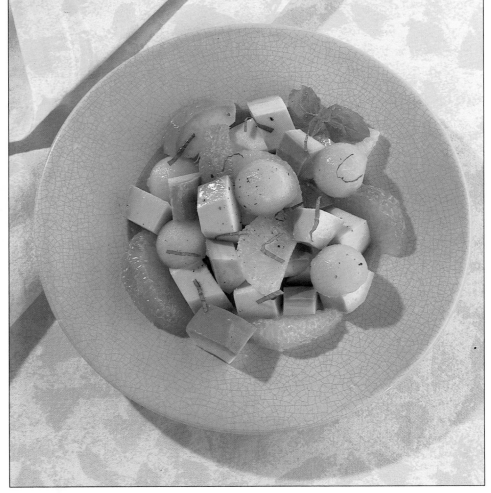

Cool and Crunchy Salad

SERVES 4

1 medium red onion, thinly sliced into rings

salt and pepper

2 navel oranges, peeled and cut in sections

1 firm jícama, peeled and cut in matchstick strips

2 heads of radicchio, cored, or 1 head of red leaf lettuce, leaves separated

3 tablespoons chopped fresh parsley

3 tablespoons chopped fresh basil

1 tablespoon white wine vinegar

¼ cup walnut oil

1 ▲ Put the onion in a colander and sprinkle with 1 teaspoon salt. Let drain 15 minutes.

2 In a mixing bowl combine the orange sections and jícama strips.

3 Spread out the radicchio or lettuce leaves on a large shallow bowl or serving platter.

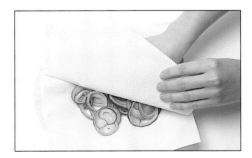

4 ▲ Rinse the onion and dry on paper towels. Toss it with the jícama and orange.

5 ▼ Arrange the jícama, orange, and onion mixture on top of the radicchio leaves. Sprinkle with the parsley and basil.

6 ▲ Combine the vinegar, oil, and salt and pepper to taste in a screwtop jar. Shake well to combine. Pour the dressing over the salad and serve immediately.

Creamy Coleslaw

SERVES 6

¾ pound green or white cabbage, cut in wedges and cored

¼ pound red cabbage, cored

3 scallions, finely chopped

2 medium carrots, grated

1 teaspoon sugar

2 tablespoons fresh lemon juice

2 teaspoons distilled white vinegar

½ cup sour cream

½ cup mayonnaise

¾ teaspoon celery seeds

salt and pepper

1 ▼ Slice the green and red cabbage thinly across the leaves.

2 Place the cabbage in a mixing bowl and add the scallions and carrots. Toss to combine.

3 In a small bowl, combine the sugar, lemon juice, vinegar, sour cream, mayonnaise, and celery seeds.

4 ▲ Pour the mayonnaise dressing over the vegetables. Season with salt and pepper. Stir until well coated. Spoon into a serving bowl.

Potato Salad

SERVES 8

3 pounds small new potatoes

2 tablespoons white wine vinegar

1 tablespoon Dijon-style mustard

3 tablespoons vegetable or olive oil

½ cup chopped red onion

salt and pepper

½ cup mayonnaise

2 tablespoons chopped fresh tarragon or 1½ teaspoons dried tarragon

½ cup thinly sliced celery

1 Cook the unpeeled potatoes in boiling salted water until tender, 15–20 minutes. Drain.

2 In a small bowl, mix together the vinegar and mustard until the mustard dissolves. Whisk in the oil.

3 ▲ When the potatoes are cool enough to handle, slice them into a large mixing bowl.

4 ▲ Add the onion to the potatoes and pour the dressing over them. Season, then toss gently to combine. Let stand at least 30 minutes.

5 ▲ Mix together the mayonnaise and tarragon. Gently stir into the potatoes, along with the celery. Taste and adjust the seasoning before serving.

~ **VARIATION** ~

Substitute 3 tablespoons dry white wine for the wine vinegar, if preferred. When available, use small red potatoes to give a nice color to the salad.

Creamy Coleslaw (top), Potato Salad

Pasta and Avocado Salad

SERVES 6

3 cups pasta spirals (fusilli) or other small pasta shapes

½ cup drained canned whole-kernel corn or frozen whole-kernel corn, thawed

½ red bell pepper, seeded and diced

8 black olives, pitted and sliced

3 scallions, finely chopped

2 medium avocados

FOR THE DRESSING

2 sun-dried tomato halves, loose-packed (not packed in oil)

1½ tablespoons balsamic vinegar

1½ tablespoons red wine vinegar

½ garlic clove, minced

½ teaspoon salt

5 tablespoons olive oil

1 tablespoon chopped fresh basil

1 ▼ For the dressing, drop the sun-dried tomatoes into a pan containing 1 inch of boiling water and simmer until tender, about 3 minutes. Drain and chop finely.

2 ▲ Combine the tomatoes, vinegars, garlic, and salt in a food processor. With the machine on, add the oil in a stream. Stir in the basil.

3 Cook the pasta in a large pan of boiling salted water until just tender to the bite (check package directions for timing). Drain well.

4 ▲ In a large bowl, combine the pasta, corn, red bell pepper, olives, and scallions. Add the dressing and toss well together.

5 ▲ Just before serving, peel the avocados and cut the flesh into cubes. Mix gently into the pasta salad, and serve at room temperature.

Ham and Black-Eyed Pea Salad

SERVES 8

1 cup dry black-eyed peas
1 onion, peeled
1 carrot, peeled
½ pound smoked ham, diced
3 medium tomatoes, peeled, seeded, and diced (about 1 cup)
salt and pepper

FOR THE DRESSING

2 garlic cloves, minced
3 tablespoons olive oil
3 tablespoons red wine vinegar
2 tablespoons corn oil
1 tablespoon fresh lemon juice
1 tablespoon chopped fresh basil or 1 teaspoon dried basil
1 tablespoon whole-grain mustard
1 teaspoon soy sauce
½ teaspoon dried oregano
½ teaspoon sugar
¼ teaspoon Worcestershire sauce
½ teaspoon hot pepper sauce

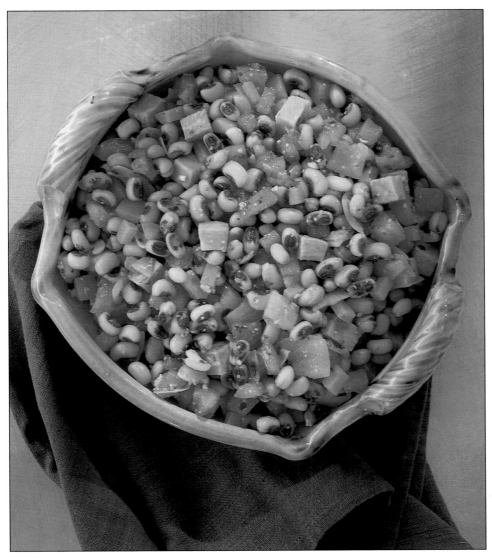

1 Soak the black-eyed peas in water to cover overnight. Drain.

2 ▲ Put the peas in a large saucepan and add the onion and carrot. Cover with fresh cold water and bring to a boil. Lower the heat and simmer until the peas are tender, about 1 hour. Drain, reserving the onion and carrot. Transfer the peas to a salad bowl.

3 ▼ Finely chop the onion and carrot. Toss with the peas. Stir in the ham and tomatoes.

4 For the dressing, combine all the ingredients in a small bowl and whisk to mix.

5 ▲ Pour the dressing over the peas. Season with salt and pepper. Toss to combine.

Scalloped Potatoes

SERVES 6–8

2½ pounds potatoes, peeled and cut in ⅛-inch slices

salt and pepper

1 large onion, thinly sliced

¼ cup flour

4 tablespoons butter or margarine, cut in small pieces

1½ cups shredded cheddar cheese

1 cup milk

2 cups light cream

1 Preheat the oven to 350°F. Butter a 14-inch oval gratin dish.

2 Layer one-quarter of the potato slices in the prepared dish. Season with salt and pepper.

3 ▼ Layer one-quarter of the sliced onion over the potatoes. Sprinkle with 1 tablespoon of the flour and dot with 2 tablespoons of the butter or margarine. Sprinkle with one-quarter of the cheese.

4 Continue layering these ingredients, making 4 layers.

5 ▲ Heat the milk and light cream in a small saucepan. Pour the mixture evenly over the potatoes.

6 Cover the gratin dish with foil. Place it in the oven and bake for 1 hour. Remove the foil and bake until the potatoes are tender and the top is golden, 15–20 minutes longer.

New Potatoes with Shallot Butter

SERVES 6

1¼ pounds small new potatoes

4 tablespoons butter or margarine

3 shallots, finely chopped

2 garlic cloves, minced

salt and pepper

1 teaspoon chopped fresh tarragon

1 teaspoon chopped fresh chives

1 teaspoon chopped fresh parsley

1 Bring a saucepan of salted water to a boil. Add the potatoes and cook until just tender, 15–20 minutes. Drain well.

2 ▼ Melt the butter or margarine in a skillet. Add the shallots and garlic and cook over low heat until softened, about 5 minutes.

3 ▲ Add the potatoes to the skillet and stir well to mix with the shallot butter. Season with salt and pepper. Cook, stirring, until the potatoes are heated through.

4 Transfer the potatoes to a warmed serving bowl. Sprinkle with the chopped herbs before serving.

Scalloped Potatoes (top), New Potatoes with Shallot Butter

Broccoli and Cauliflower Mold

SERVES 6

1–1½ pounds broccoli, stems trimmed

1–1½ pounds cauliflower, stems trimmed

FOR THE CHEESE SAUCE

3 tablespoons butter or margarine

¼ cup flour

1½ cups milk

¾ cup shredded cheddar cheese

⅛ teaspoon grated nutmeg

salt and pepper

1 Preheat the oven to 300°F. Butter a 1-quart ovenproof bowl or round mold.

2 Break the broccoli into florets. Drop into a pan of boiling salted water and cook 5 minutes. Drain and rinse with cold water to stop the cooking. Drain thoroughly, then spread on paper towels to dry.

3 Break the cauliflower into florets. Drop into a pan of boiling salted water and cook 5 minutes. Drain and rinse with cold water. Drain thoroughly, then spread on paper towels to dry.

4 ▲ Place a cluster of cauliflower on the bottom of the prepared bowl, stems pointing inwards. Add a layer of broccoli, buds against the side and stems pointing inwards. Fill the center with smaller florets.

5 ▲ Add another layer of cauliflower florets. Finish with a layer of broccoli.

6 Cover the mold with buttered foil. Bake until the vegetables are heated through, 10–15 minutes.

7 Meanwhile, for the sauce, melt the butter or margarine in a saucepan. Add the flour and cook 2 minutes, stirring. Stir in the milk. Bring to a boil, stirring constantly, and simmer until thickened, about 5 minutes. Stir in the cheese. Season with the nutmeg and salt and pepper to taste. Keep the sauce warm over very low heat.

8 ▲ Hold a warmed serving plate over the top of the bowl, turn them over together, and lift off the bowl. Serve the molded vegetables with the cheese sauce.

Green Bean and Red Bell Pepper Stir-Fry

SERVES 4

1 pound green beans, cut diagonally in 1-inch pieces

2 tablespoons olive oil

1 red bell pepper, seeded and cut in matchstick strips

½ teaspoon soy sauce

1 teaspoon fresh lemon juice

1 Drop the green beans into a pan of boiling salted water and cook 3 minutes. Drain and refresh in cold water. Blot dry with paper towels.

2 ▼ Heat the oil in a frying pan. Add the green beans and red bell pepper and stir-fry until crisp-tender, about 2 minutes.

3 ▲ Remove the pan from the heat and stir in the soy sauce and lemon juice. Transfer the vegetables to a warmed serving dish.

Broccoli and Cauliflower Mold (top), Green Bean and Red Bell Pepper Stir-Fry

Braised Red Cabbage with Apples

SERVES 6

2-pound head of red cabbage, quartered and cored

salt and pepper

2 medium red onions, peeled, halved, and thinly sliced

2 Red Delicious apples, peeled, cored, halved, and thinly sliced

1½ teaspoons caraway seeds

3 tablespoons light brown sugar

3 tablespoons red wine vinegar

2 tablespoons butter or margarine, diced

1 Preheat the oven to 400°F.

2 Slice the cabbage quarters thinly across the leaves.

~ **VARIATION** ~

For a sharper flavor, substitute Granny Smith, Greening or other tart varieties for the Red Delicious apples in this recipe.

3 ▲ Make a layer of one-quarter of the cabbage in a large, deep baking dish. Season with salt and pepper.

4 ▲ Layer one-third of the sliced onions and apples on top of the cabbage. Sprinkle with some of the caraway seeds and 1 tablespoon of the brown sugar.

5 Continue layering until all the ingredients have been used, ending with a layer of cabbage on top.

6 ▲ Pour in the vinegar and dot the top with the butter or margarine. Cover and bake 1 hour.

7 Remove the cover and continue baking until the cabbage is very tender and all the liquid has evaporated, about 30 minutes longer.

Glazed Carrots and Scallions

SERVES 6

1 pound baby carrots, trimmed and peeled if necessary

1½ tablespoons butter or margarine

2 tablespoons honey

2 tablespoons fresh orange juice

½ pound scallions, cut diagonally into 1-inch pieces

salt and pepper

1 Cook the carrots in boiling salted water or steam them until just tender, about 10 minutes. Drain if necessary.

2 ▼ In a skillet, melt the butter or margarine with the honey and orange juice, stirring until the mixture is smooth and well combined.

3 ▲ Add the carrots and scallions to the skillet. Cook over medium heat, stirring occasionally, until the vegetables are heated through and glazed, about 5 minutes. Season with salt and pepper before serving.

Braised Red Cabbage with Apples (top), Glazed Carrots and Scallions

Baked Onions with Sun-Dried Tomatoes

SERVES 4

1 pound pearl onions, peeled

2 teaspoons chopped fresh rosemary or
  ¾ teaspoon dried rosemary

2 garlic cloves, chopped

1 tablespoon chopped fresh parsley

salt and pepper

½ cup sun-dried tomatoes packed in oil,
  drained and chopped

6 tablespoons olive oil

1 tablespoon white wine vinegar

1 Preheat the oven to 300°F. Grease
a shallow baking dish.

2 ▼ Drop the onions into a pan of
boiling water and cook 5 minutes.
Drain in a colander.

3 ▲ Spread the onions in the bottom
of the prepared baking dish.

4 ▲ Combine the rosemary, garlic,
parsley, salt, and pepper and sprinkle
over the onions.

5 ▲ Scatter the tomatoes over the
onions. Drizzle the olive oil and
vinegar on top.

6 Cover with a sheet of foil and bake
45 minutes, basting occasionally.
Remove the foil and bake until the
onions are golden, about 15 minutes
longer.

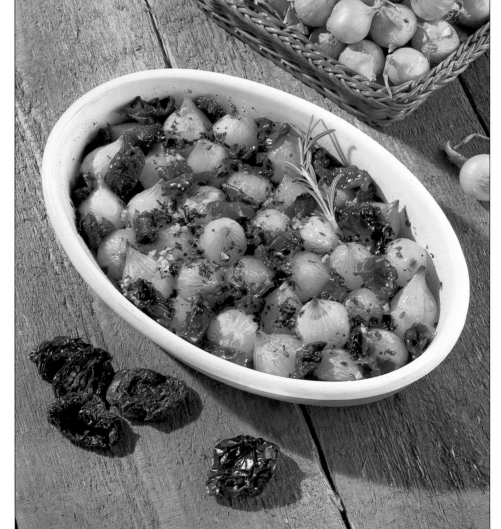

Stewed Tomatoes

SERVES 6

2 pounds very ripe tomatoes, stems removed
2 tablespoons butter or margarine
2 celery stalks, diced
1 small green bell pepper, seeded and diced
2 scallions, finely chopped
salt and pepper
2 tablespoons chopped fresh basil

1 Fill a mixing bowl with boiling water and another bowl with ice water. Three or four at a time, drop the tomatoes into the boiling water and leave them 30 seconds.

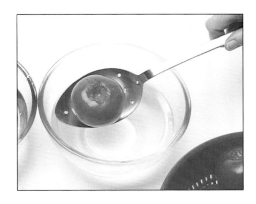

2 ▲ Remove the tomatoes with a slotted spoon and transfer to the ice water. When they are cool enough to handle, remove the tomatoes from the ice water.

3 ▲ Peel the tomatoes and cut them into wedges.

4 ▼ Heat the butter or margarine in a flameproof casserole or saucepan. Add the celery, green bell pepper, and scallions and cook until softened, about 5 minutes.

~ **VARIATION** ~

To make stewed tomatoes into a tomato sauce, cook uncovered in a shallow pan such as a skillet until thickened to the desired consistency.

5 ▲ Stir in the tomatoes. Cover and cook until the tomatoes are soft but not mushy, 10–15 minutes, stirring occasionally. Season with salt and pepper.

6 Remove the pan from the heat and stir in the basil.

Spanish Omelet

SERVES 4

4 bacon slices

3 tablespoons olive oil

1 onion, thinly sliced

½ small red bell pepper, seeded and sliced

½ small green bell pepper, seeded and sliced

1 large garlic clove, minced

¾ pound small round potatoes, cooked and sliced

4 eggs

2 tablespoons light cream

salt and pepper

1 Preheat the oven to 350°F.

2 In a heavy 8-inch skillet with an ovenproof handle, fry the bacon until crisp. Drain on paper towels.

3 Pour off the bacon fat from the skillet. Add 1 tablespoon oil to the pan and cook the onion and bell peppers until softened, about 5 minutes.

4 ▲ Remove the skillet from the heat and stir in the garlic. Crumble in the bacon. Reserve the mixture in a bowl until needed.

5 ▲ Heat the remaining oil in the skillet. Lay the potato slices in the bottom of the pan, slightly overlapping. Spoon the bacon, onion, and bell pepper mixture evenly over the potatoes.

6 In a small bowl, beat together the eggs, cream, and salt and pepper to taste.

7 ▲ Pour the egg mixture into the skillet. Cook over low heat until the egg is set, lifting the edge of the omelette with a knife several times to let the uncooked egg seep down.

8 Transfer the skillet to the oven to finish cooking the omelet, 5–10 minutes longer. Serve hot or warm, cut into wedges.

Spinach and Cheese Pie

Serves 8

3 pounds fresh spinach, coarse stems removed

2 tablespoons olive oil

1 medium onion, finely chopped

2 tablespoons chopped fresh oregano or 1 teaspoon dried oregano

4 eggs

2 cups creamed cottage cheese

6 tablespoons freshly grated Parmesan cheese

grated nutmeg

salt and pepper

12 sheets of phyllo pastry

4 tablespoons butter or margarine, melted

1 Preheat the oven to 375°F.

2 ▲ Stack handfuls of spinach leaves, roll them loosely, and cut across the leaves into thin ribbons.

3 Heat the oil in a large saucepan. Add the onion and cook until softened, about 5 minutes.

4 Add the spinach and oregano and cook over high heat until most of liquid from the spinach evaporates, about 5 minutes, stirring frequently. Remove from the heat and let cool.

5 Break the eggs into a bowl and beat. Stir in the cottage cheese and Parmesan cheese, and season generously with nutmeg, salt, and pepper. Stir in the spinach mixture.

6 ▲ Brush a 13- × 9-inch baking dish with some of the butter or margarine. Arrange half of the phyllo sheets in the bottom of the dish to cover evenly and extend about 1 inch up the sides. Brush with butter.

7 ▲ Ladle in the spinach and cheese filling. Cover with the remaining phyllo pastry, tucking under the edge neatly.

8 Brush the top with the remaining butter. Score the top with diamond shapes using a sharp knife.

9 Bake until the pastry is golden brown, about 30 minutes. Cut into squares and serve hot.

Asparagus, Corn, and Red Bell Pepper Quiche

SERVES 6

½ pound fresh asparagus, woody stalks removed

2 tablespoons butter or margarine

1 small onion, finely chopped

1 red bell pepper, seeded and finely chopped

½ cup drained canned corn or frozen corn, thawed

2 eggs

1 cup light cream

½ cup shredded cheddar cheese

salt and pepper

FOR THE CRUST

1⅔ cups flour

½ teaspoon salt

½ cup shortening

2–3 tablespoons ice water

1 Preheat the oven to 400°F.

2 For the crust, sift the flour and salt into a mixing bowl. Using a pastry blender, cut in the shortening until the mixture resembles coarse crumbs. Sprinkle in the water, 1 tablespoon at a time, tossing lightly with your fingertips or a fork until the dough will form a ball.

3 ▲ On a lightly floured surface, roll out the dough. Use it to line a 10-inch quiche dish or loose-bottomed tart pan, easing the dough in and being careful not to stretch it. Trim off excess dough.

4 ▲ Line the pie shell with wax paper and weigh it down with pie weights or dry beans. Bake 10 minutes. Remove the paper and weights or beans and bake until the pastry shell is set and beige in color, about 5 minutes longer. Let cool.

5 Trim the stem ends of 8 of the asparagus spears to make them 4 inches in length. Set aside.

6 ▲ Finely chop the asparagus trimmings and any remaining spears. Place in the bottom of the pie shell.

7 ▲ Melt the butter or margarine in a frying pan. Add the onion and red bell pepper and cook until softened, about 5 minutes. Stir in the corn and cook 2 minutes longer.

8 Spoon the corn mixture over the chopped asparagus in the pie shell.

9 ▲ In a small bowl, beat the eggs with the cream. Stir in the cheese and salt and pepper to taste. Pour into the pie shell.

10 ▲ Arrange the reserved asparagus spears like the spokes of a wheel on top of the filling.

11 Bake until the filling is set, 25–30 minutes.

~ VARIATION ~

To make individual tartlets, roll out the dough and use to line 12 3-inch tartlet molds. For the filling, cut off and reserve the asparagus tips and chop the tender part of the stalks. Mix the asparagus and the cooked vegetables into the egg mixture with the cheese. Spoon the filling into the molds and bake as directed, decreasing baking time by about 8–10 minutes.

Cheesy Bread Pudding

SERVES 4

3 tablespoons butter or margarine, at room temperature

2½ cups milk

3 eggs, beaten

½ cup freshly grated Parmesan cheese

⅛ teaspoon cayenne

salt and pepper

5 large, thick slices of crusty white bread

2 cups shredded cheddar cheese

1 Grease an oval baking dish with the butter or margarine.

2 ▼ In a bowl combine the milk, eggs, 3 tablespoons of the Parmesan cheese, the cayenne, and salt and pepper to taste.

3 ▲ Cut the bread slices in half. Arrange 5 of them in the bottom of the prepared dish, overlapping the slices if necessary.

4 ▲ Sprinkle the bread with two-thirds of the cheddar cheese. Top with the remaining bread.

5 Pour the egg mixture evenly over the bread. Press the bread down gently so that it will absorb the egg mixture. Sprinkle the top evenly with the remaining Parmesan and cheddar cheeses. Let stand until the bread has absorbed most of the egg mixture, at least 30 minutes.

6 Preheat the oven to 425°F.

7 Set the baking dish in a roasting pan. Add enough boiling water to the pan to come halfway up the sides of the baking dish.

8 Place in the oven and bake 30 minutes, or until the pudding is lightly set and browned. If the pudding browns too quickly, before setting, cover loosely with foil. Serve hot.

Tomato and Basil Tartlets

MAKES 12–18

2 eggs
3 tablespoons whipping cream
3 tablespoons crumbled feta cheese
salt and pepper
½ pound tomatoes, peeled, seeded, and chopped
12 fresh basil leaves, cut in thin ribbons
FOR THE CRUST
1 ⅔ cups flour
½ teaspoon salt
½ cup shortening
2–3 tablespoons ice water

1 Preheat the oven to 400°F.

2 For the crust, sift the flour and salt into a mixing bowl. Using a pastry blender, cut in the shortening until the mixture resembles coarse crumbs. Sprinkle in the water, 1 tablespoon at a time, tossing lightly with your fingertips or a fork until the dough will form a ball.

3 ▲ On a lightly floured surface, roll out the dough thinly. With a fluted 2½-inch cookie cutter, cut out 18 rounds. Use the rounds to line 18 cups in mini-muffin pans. (Muffin pans vary in size. Cut out larger rounds, if necessary, and make fewer tartlets.)

4 In a bowl, combine the eggs and cream and beat together. Stir in the cheese and salt and pepper to taste.

5 ▼ In a small saucepan, warm the tomatoes with the basil. Drain the tomatoes, then stir them into the egg mixture.

6 ▲ Divide the tomato mixture evenly among the tartlet shells. Bake 10 minutes. Reduce the heat to 350°F and bake until the filling has set and the pastry is golden brown, about 10 minutes longer. Let cool on a wire rack before serving.

Bulgur Wheat Salad

SERVES 6

⅔ cup fine bulgur wheat

1 cup water

1½ cups finely chopped fresh parsley

¼ cup chopped fresh mint or 2 tablespoons dried mint

¼ cup finely chopped scallions

¼ cup finely chopped red onion

1 large tomato, chopped

¼ cup olive oil

⅓ cup fresh lemon juice

salt and pepper

½ head of romaine lettuce, leaves separated

1 Place the bulgur wheat in a bowl. Pour the water over the wheat. Let stand until the wheat swells and softens, about 30 minutes.

2 ▲ A handful at a time, squeeze excess water out of the bulgur wheat and put it in a mixing bowl.

3 ▲ Add the parsley, mint, scallions, red onion, and tomato to the bulgur wheat. Stir in the olive oil and lemon juice. Season to taste.

4 Line a large serving platter with romaine leaves. Pile the bulgur wheat salad in the middle.

Hot Cheesy Grits

SERVES 6

3 cups water

¼ teaspoon salt

¾ cup instant grits

1 egg

1½ cups shredded cheddar or Monterey Jack cheese

2 tablespoons butter or margarine

⅛ teaspoon cayenne

1 Preheat the oven to 350°F. Grease a 13- × 9-inch baking dish.

2 Put the water and salt in a medium saucepan and bring to a boil.

~ COOK'S TIP ~

Try this Southern specialty for breakfast or brunch, or in place of rice or potatoes to accompany a main course.

3 ▲ Stir in the grits. Reduce the heat to low, cover the pan, and cook the grits until thickened, 5–7 minutes, stirring occasionally.

4 ▲ In a small bowl, beat the egg lightly. Add a large spoonful of the cooked grits and stir well to mix.

5 Stir the egg mixture into the remaining cooked grits in the saucepan. Add 1 cup of the cheese, the butter, and the cayenne. Stir over low heat until the cheese melts.

6 ▲ Transfer the mixture to the prepared dish. Sprinkle the remaining cheese over the top. Bake until the cheesy grits are set and golden on top, 35–40 minutes. Let cool 5 minutes before cutting and serving.

Bulgur Wheat Salad (top), Hot Cheesy Grits

Fried Rice with Asparagus and Shrimp

SERVES 4

3 tablespoons corn oil

¾ pound asparagus, cut diagonally into 1-inch lengths (1½ cups)

1 cup sliced fresh shiitake mushrooms

3 cups cooked rice

1 teaspoon finely grated fresh gingerroot

½ pound cooked peeled shrimp, deveined

½ cup sliced canned water chestnuts, drained

3 tablespoons soy sauce

pepper

~ VARIATION ~

Ingredients for fried rice are infinately variable. Instead of shrimp, try scallops or cubes of firm-fleshed fish. Replace water chestnuts with a crunchy vegetable, such as snow peas.

1 ▲ Heat the oil in a wok over high heat. Add the asparagus and mushrooms and stir-fry, 3–4 minutes.

2 ▲ Stir in the rice and gingerroot. Cook, stirring, until heated through, about 3 minutes.

3 ▲ Add the shrimp and stir-fry for 1 minute.

4 ▲ Add the water chestnuts and soy sauce and stir-fry 1 minute longer. Season with pepper and serve.

Saffron Rice

SERVES 6

4 tablespoons butter or margarine

⅛ teaspoon saffron threads

2½ cups long-grain rice

4 cups chicken stock

½ teaspoon salt

~ COOK'S TIP ~

If preferred, cook the saffron rice in a preheated 375°F oven, in a flameproof casserole. Bring to a boil, then transfer to the oven.

1 Melt the butter or margarine in a large saucepan. Stir in the saffron.

2 ▲ Add the rice and stir to coat all the grains well with the saffron butter.

3 ▼ Stir in the stock and salt. Bring to a boil. Reduce the heat to low, cover, and simmer until the rice is tender and all the stock has been absorbed, about 20 minutes.

4 Fluff the rice grains with a fork before serving.

Fried Rice with Asparagus and Shrimp (top), Saffron Rice

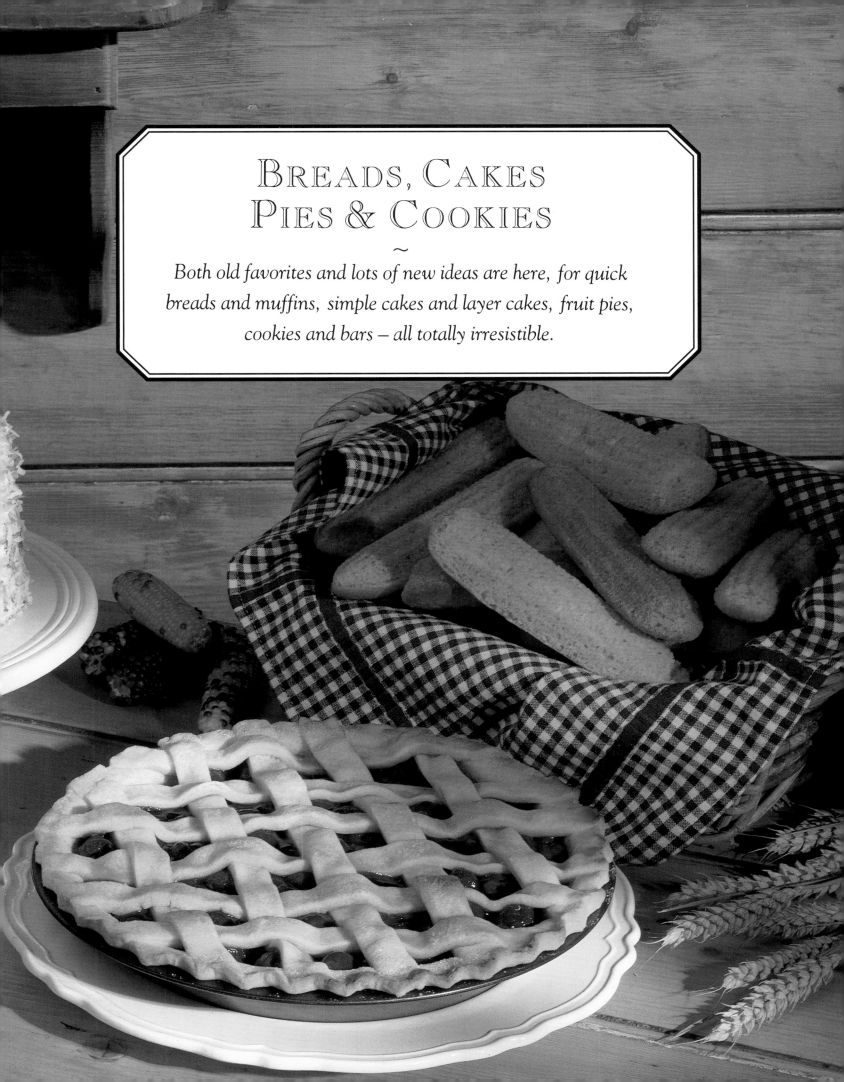

BREADS, CAKES
PIES & COOKIES

~

*Both old favorites and lots of new ideas are here, for quick
breads and muffins, simple cakes and layer cakes, fruit pies,
cookies and bars – all totally irresistible.*

Coconut Angel Food Cake

Serves 10

1½ cups confectioners' sugar
1 cup cake flour
1½ cups egg whites (about 12 egg whites)
1½ teaspoons cream of tartar
1 cup granulated sugar
¼ teaspoon salt
2 teaspoons almond extract
1 cup flaked coconut
FOR THE FROSTING
2 egg whites
½ cup granulated sugar
¼ teaspoon salt
2 tablespoons cold water
2 teaspoons almond extract
2 cups flaked coconut, toasted

3 ▲ Continue beating until stiff and glossy. Swiftly beat in the reserved 2 tablespoons of sugar, along with the salt and almond extract.

4 ▲ Using a ¼-cup measure, sprinkle the flour mixture over the meringue, quickly folding until just combined. Fold in the flaked coconut in 2 batches.

5 ▲ Transfer the batter to an ungreased 10-inch angel cake pan, and cut gently through the batter with a metal spatula. Bake until the top of the cake springs back when touched lightly, 30–35 minutes.

6 ▲ As soon as the cake is done, turn the pan upside down and suspend its funnel over the neck of a funnel or bottle. Let cool, about 1 hour.

7 ▲ For the frosting, combine the egg whites, sugar, salt, and water in a heatproof bowl. Beat with an electric mixer until blended. Set the bowl over a pan of boiling water and continue beating on medium speed until the frosting is stiff, about 3 minutes. Remove the pan from the heat and stir in the almond extract.

8 ▲ Unmold the cake onto a serving plate. Spread the frosting gently over the top and sides of the cake. Sprinkle with the toasted coconut.

1 ▲ Preheat the oven to 350°F. Sift the confectioners' sugar and flour into a bowl. Set aside.

2 With an electric mixer, beat the egg whites with the cream of tartar on medium speed until very thick. Turn the mixer to high speed and beat in the granulated sugar, 2 tablespoons at a time, reserving 2 tablespoons.

Carrot Cake with Cream Cheese Frosting

SERVES 10

2 cups granulated sugar

1 cup vegetable oil

4 eggs

2 cups finely grated carrots
    (about ½ pound)

2 cups flour

1½ teaspoons baking soda

1½ teaspoons baking powder

1 teaspoon ground allspice

1 teaspoon ground cinnamon

FOR THE FROSTING

2 cups confectioners' sugar

1 8-ounce package cream cheese, at
    room temperature

4 tablespoons butter or margarine, at
    room temperature

2 teaspoons vanilla extract

1½ cups walnut pieces or pecans,
    chopped

1 Preheat the oven to 375°F. Butter and flour 2 9-inch round cake pans.

2 ▲ In a mixing bowl, combine the granulated sugar, vegetable oil, eggs, and carrots.

3 Sift the dry ingredients into another bowl. Add by ½-cup measures to the carrot mixture, mixing well after each addition.

4 ▲ Divide the batter evenly between the prepared cake pans. Bake until a cake tester inserted in the center comes out clean, 35–40 minutes.

5 Let cool in the pans on wire racks for 10 minutes, then unmold the cakes from the pans onto the wire racks and let cool completely.

6 For the frosting, combine everything but the nuts in a bowl and beat until smooth.

7 ▲ To assemble, set 1 cake layer on a serving plate and spread with one-third of the frosting. Place the second cake layer on top. Spread the remaining frosting all over the top and sides of the cake, swirling it to make a decorative finish. Sprinkle the nuts around the top edge.

Apple and Pear Skillet Cake

SERVES 6

1 apple, peeled, cored, and thinly sliced
1 pear, peeled, cored, and thinly sliced
½ cup walnut pieces, chopped
1 teaspoon ground cinnamon
1 teaspoon grated nutmeg
3 eggs
¾ cup flour
2 tablespoons light brown sugar, firmly packed
¾ cup milk
1 teaspoon vanilla extract
4 tablespoons butter or margarine
confectioners' sugar, for sprinkling

1 ▲ Preheat the oven to 375°F. In a mixing bowl, toss together the apple slices, pear slices, walnuts, cinnamon, and nutmeg. Set aside.

3 ▼ Melt the butter or margarine in a 9- or 10-inch ovenproof skillet (preferably castiron) over medium heat. Add the apple mixture. Cook until lightly caramelized, about 5 minutes, stirring occasionally.

2 ▲ With an electric mixer, beat together the eggs, flour, brown sugar, milk, and vanilla.

4 ▲ Pour the batter over the fruit and nuts. Transfer the skillet to the oven and bake until the cake is puffy and pulling away from the sides of the pan, about 30 minutes.

5 Sprinkle the cake lightly with confectioners' sugar and serve hot.

Devil's Food Cake

Serves 10

4 1-ounce squares semisweet chocolate
1¼ cups milk
1 cup light brown sugar, firmly packed
1 egg yolk
2¼ cups cake flour
1 teaspoon baking soda
½ teaspoon salt
⅔ cup (10⅔ tablespoons) butter or margarine, at room temperature
1⅓ cups granulated sugar
3 eggs
1 teaspoon vanilla extract
For the frosting
8 1-ounce squares semisweet chocolate
¾ cup sour cream
¼ teaspoon salt

7 Divide the batter evenly between the cake pans. Bake until a cake tester inserted in the center comes out clean, 30–40 minutes.

2 ▲ In a heatproof bowl set over a pan of simmering water, or in a double boiler, combine the chocolate, ½ cup of the milk, the brown sugar, and egg yolk. Cook, stirring, until smooth and thickened. Let cool.

3 ▲ Sift the flour, baking soda, and salt into a small bowl. Set aside.

4 ▲ With an electric mixer, cream the butter or margarine with the granulated sugar until light and fluffy. Beat in the whole eggs, one at a time. Mix in the vanilla.

5 On low speed, beat the flour mixture into the butter mixture alternately with the remaining milk, beginning and ending with flour.

6 ▲ Pour in the chocolate mixture and mix until just combined.

7 Divide the batter evenly between the cake pans. Bake until a cake tester inserted in the center comes out clean, 25–30 minutes.

8 Let cool in the pans on wire racks for 10 minutes, then unmold the cakes from the pans onto the wire racks and let cool completely.

9 ▲ For the frosting, melt the chocolate in a heatproof bowl set over a pan of hot, not boiling, water, or in the top of a double boiler. Remove the bowl from the heat and stir in the sour cream and salt. Let cool slightly.

10 ▲ Set 1 cake layer on a serving plate and spread with one-third of the frosting. Place the second cake layer on top. Spread the remaining frosting all over the top and sides of the cake, swirling it to make a decorative finish.

Mississippi Mud Pie

SERVES 8

3 1-ounce squares semisweet chocolate

4 tablespoons butter or margarine

3 tablespoons corn syrup

3 eggs, beaten

⅔ cup sugar

1 teaspoon vanilla extract

4-oz chocolate bar

2 cups whipping cream

FOR THE CRUST

1⅓ cups flour

½ teaspoon salt

½ cup shortening

2–3 tablespoons ice water

1 Preheat the oven to 425°F.

2 For the crust, sift the flour and salt into a mixing bowl. Using a pastry blender, cut in the shortening until the mixture resembles coarse crumbs. Sprinkle in the water, 1 tablespoon at a time. Toss lightly with your fingers or a fork until the dough will form a ball.

3 On a lightly floured surface, roll out the dough. Use to line an 8- or 9-inch pie pan, easing in the dough and being careful not to stretch it. With your thumbs, make a fluted edge.

4 Using a fork, prick the bottom and sides of the pie shell all over. Bake until lightly browned, 10–15 minutes. Let cool, in the pan, on a wire rack.

5 ▲ In a heatproof bowl set over a pan of simmering water, or in a double boiler, melt 3 squares of chocolate, the butter or margarine, and corn syrup. Remove the bowl from the heat and stir in the eggs, sugar, and vanilla.

6 Reduce the oven temperature to 350°F. Pour the chocolate mixture into the baked crust. Bake until the filling is set, 35–40 minutes. Let cool completely in the pan, set on a rack.

7 ▲ For the decoration, use the heat of your hands to slightly soften the chocolate bar. Draw the blade of a swivel-headed vegetable peeler along the side of the chocolate bar to shave off short, wide curls. Chill the chocolate curls until needed.

8 Before serving, lightly whip the cream until soft peaks form. Using a rubber spatula, spread the cream over the surface of the chocolate filling. Decorate with the chocolate curls.

Banana Cream Pie

SERVES 6

2 cups finely crushed gingersnaps
5 tablespoons butter or margarine, melted
½ teaspoon grated nutmeg or ground cinnamon
¾ cup mashed ripe bananas
1½ 8-ounce packages cream cheese, at room temperature
¼ cup thick plain yogurt or sour cream
3 tablespoons dark rum or 1 teaspoon vanilla extract
FOR THE TOPPING
1 cup whipping cream
3–4 bananas

1 Preheat the oven to 375°F.

2 ▲ In a mixing bowl, combine the cookie crumbs, butter or margarine, and spice. Mix thoroughly with a wooden spoon.

3 ▲ Press the cookie mixture into a 9-inch pie pan, building up thick sides with a neat edge. Bake 5 minutes. Let cool, in the pan, on a wire rack.

4 ▼ With an electric mixer, beat the mashed bananas with the cream cheese. Fold in the yogurt or sour cream and rum or vanilla. Spread the filling in the crumb crust. Refrigerate at least 4 hours or overnight.

5 ▲ For the topping, whip the cream until soft peaks form. Spread on the pie filling. Slice the bananas and arrange on top in a decorative pattern.

Cherry Lattice Pie

SERVES 8

4 cups sour cherries, pitted (2 pounds fresh or 2 16-ounce cans, water-pack, drained)

⅓ cup sugar

¼ cup flour

1½ tablespoons fresh lemon juice

¼ teaspoon almond extract

2 tablespoons butter or margarine

FOR THE CRUST

2 cups flour

1 teaspoon salt

¾ cup shortening

4–5 tablespoons ice water

1 For the crust, sift the flour and salt into a mixing bowl. Using a pastry blender, cut in the shortening until the mixture resembles coarse crumbs.

2 ▲ Sprinkle in the water, 1 tablespoon at a time, tossing lightly with your fingertips or a fork until the dough will form a ball.

3 Divide the dough in half and shape each half into a ball. On a lightly floured surface, roll out one of the balls to a circle about 12 inches in diameter.

4 ▲ Use it to line a 9-inch pie pan, easing the dough in and being careful not to stretch it. With scissors, trim off excess dough, leaving a ½-inch overhang around the pie rim.

5 ▲ Roll out the remaining dough to ⅛-inch thickness. With a sharp knife, cut out 11 strips ½ inch wide.

6 ▲ In a mixing bowl, combine the cherries, sugar, flour, lemon juice, and almond extract. Spoon the mixture into the pie crust and dot with the butter or margarine.

7 ▲ To make the lattice, place 5 of the pastry-dough strips evenly across the filling. Fold every other strip back. Lay the first strip across in the opposite direction. Continue in this pattern, folding back every other strip each time you add a cross strip.

8 ▲ Trim the ends of the lattice strips even with the crust overhang. Press together so that the edge rests on the pie-pan rim. With your thumbs, flute the edge. Refrigerate 15 minutes.

9 Preheat the oven to 425°F.

10 Bake the pie 30 minutes, covering the edge of the crust with foil, if necessary, to prevent overbrowning. Let cool, in the pan, on a wire rack.

Corn Bread

MAKES 9

2 eggs, lightly beaten

1 cup buttermilk

1 cup flour

1 cup cornmeal

2 teaspoons baking powder

½ teaspoon salt

1 tablespoon sugar

1 cup shredded sharp cheddar cheese

1 cup corn kernels, cut from 2 ears of fresh corn or thawed if frozen

~ VARIATION ~

For a spicy cornbread, stir 2 tablespoons chopped jalapeño peppers into the batter after adding the cheese and corn.

1 Preheat the oven to 400°F. Grease a 9-inch square baking pan.

2 Combine the eggs and buttermilk in a small bowl and whisk until well combined. Set aside.

3 ▼ In another bowl, stir together the flour, cornmeal, baking powder, salt, and sugar. Pour in the egg mixture and stir with a wooden spoon until just combined. Stir in the cheese and corn.

4 ▲ Pour the batter into the prepared pan. Bake until a cake tester inserted in the center comes out clean, about 25 minutes.

5 Unmold the cornbread onto a wire rack and let cool. Cut into 3-inch squares for serving.

Crunchy Corn Sticks

MAKES 6

1 egg

½ cup milk

1 tablespoon corn oil

1 cup cornmeal

½ cup flour

2 teaspoons baking powder

3 tablespoons sugar

~ VARIATION ~

Fry 3 strips of bacon until crisp. Drain, then crumble and mix into the batter before baking.

1 Preheat the oven to 375°F. Grease a castiron corn-stick mold.

2 Beat the egg in a small bowl. Stir in the milk and oil. Set aside.

3 ▼ In a mixing bowl, stir together the cornmeal, flour, baking powder, and sugar. Pour in the egg mixture and stir with a wooden spoon until just combined.

4 ▲ Spoon the batter into the prepared mold. Bake until a cake tester inserted in the center of a corn stick comes out clean, about 25 minutes. Let cool in the mold on a wire rack for 10 minutes before unmolding.

Corn Bread (top), Crunchy Corn Sticks

Old-Fashioned Sugar Cookies

MAKES 36

3 cups flour

1 teaspoon baking soda

2 teaspoons baking powder

¼ teaspoon grated nutmeg

½ cup (1 stick) butter or margarine, at room temperature

1 cup sugar

½ teaspoon vanilla extract

1 egg

½ cup milk

colored sugar, for sprinkling

1 Sift the flour, baking soda, baking powder, and nutmeg into a small bowl. Set aside.

2 ▲ With an electric mixer, cream the butter or margarine, sugar, and vanilla together until the mixture is light and fluffy. Add the egg and beat to mix well.

3 ▲ Add the flour mixture alternately with the milk, stirring with a wooden spoon to make a soft dough. Wrap the dough in plastic wrap and refrigerate at least 30 minutes, or overnight.

4 ▲ Preheat the oven to 350°F. Roll out the dough on a lightly floured surface to ⅛-inch thickness. Cut into rounds or other shapes with cookie cutters.

5 ▲ Transfer the cookies to ungreased cookie sheets. Sprinkle each cookie with colored sugar.

6 Bake until golden brown, 10–12 minutes. With a slotted spatula, transfer the cookies to a wire rack and let cool.

Hazelnut Brownies

MAKES 9

2 1-ounce squares unsweetened chocolate

5 tablespoons butter or margarine

1 cup sugar

7 tablespoons flour

½ teaspoon baking powder

2 eggs, beaten

½ teaspoon vanilla extract

1 cup skinned hazelnuts, roughly chopped

1 Preheat the oven to 350°F. Grease an 8-inch square baking pan.

2 ▲ In a heatproof bowl set over a pan of barely simmering water, or in a double boiler, melt the chocolate and butter or margarine. Remove the bowl from the heat.

3 ▲ Add the sugar, flour, baking powder, eggs, vanilla, and ½ cup of the hazelnuts to the melted mixture and stir well with a wooden spoon.

4 ▼ Pour the batter into the prepared pan. Bake 10 minutes, then sprinkle the reserved hazelnuts over the top. Return to the oven and continue baking until firm to the touch, about 25 minutes.

5 ▲ Let cool in the pan, set on a wire rack for 10 minutes, then unmold onto the rack and let cool completely. Cut into squares for serving.

Pepper-Spice Cookies

MAKES 48

1¾ cups flour

½ cup cornstarch

2 teaspoons baking powder

½ teaspoon ground cardamom

½ teaspoon ground cinnamon

½ teaspoon grated nutmeg

½ teaspoon ground ginger

½ teaspoon ground allspice

½ teaspoon salt

½ teaspoon freshly ground black pepper

1 cup (2 sticks) butter or margarine, at room temperature

½ cup light brown sugar, firmly packed

½ teaspoon vanilla extract

1 teaspoon finely grated lemon rind

¼ cup whipping cream

⅔ cup finely ground almonds

2 tablespoons confectioners' sugar

1 Preheat the oven to 350°F.

2 Sift the flour, cornstarch, baking powder, spices, salt, and pepper into a bowl. Set aside.

3 With an electric mixer, cream the butter or margarine and brown sugar together until light and fluffy. Beat in the vanilla and lemon rind.

4 ▲ With the mixer on low speed, add the flour mixture alternately with the cream, beginning and ending with flour. Stir in the ground almonds.

5 ▲ Shape the dough into ¾-inch balls. Place them on ungreased cookie sheets about 1 inch apart. Bake until the cookies are golden brown underneath, 15–20 minutes.

6 Let the cookies cool on the cookie sheets about 1 minute before transferring them to a wire rack to cool completely. Before serving, sprinkle them lightly with confectioners' sugar.

Five-Layer Bars

MAKES 24

2 cups graham cracker crumbs

¼ cup sugar

⅛ teaspoon salt

½ cup (1 stick) butter or margarine, melted

1 cup shredded coconut

1½ cups semisweet chocolate chips

1 cup sweetened condensed milk

1 cup walnut pieces, chopped

1 Preheat the oven to 350°F.

2 ▼ In a bowl, combine the graham-cracker crumbs, sugar, salt, and butter or margarine. Press the mixture evenly over the bottom of an ungreased 13- × 9-inch baking dish.

3 ▲ Sprinkle the coconut over the crumb crust, then scatter over the chocolate chips. Pour the condensed milk evenly over the chocolate. Sprinkle the walnuts on top.

4 Bake 30 minutes. Unmold onto a wire rack and let cool, preferably overnight. When cooled, cut into bars.

Pepper-Spice Cookies (top), Five-Layer Bars

Gingersnaps

MAKES 60

2½ cups flour

1 teaspoon baking soda

1½ teaspoons ground ginger

¼ teaspoon ground cinnamon

¼ teaspoon ground cloves

½ cup (1 stick) butter or margarine, at room temperature

1½ cups sugar

1 egg, beaten

¼ cup molasses

1 teaspoon fresh lemon juice

1 Preheat the oven to 350°F. Grease 3–4 cookie sheets.

2 Sift the flour, baking soda, ginger, cinnamon, and cloves into a small bowl. Set aside.

3 With an electric mixer, cream the butter or margarine and 1 cup of the sugar together.

4 ▲ Stir in the egg, molasses, and lemon juice. Add the flour mixture and mix in thoroughly with a wooden spoon to make a soft dough.

5 ▲ Shape the dough into ¾-inch balls. Roll the balls in the remaining sugar and place about 2 inches apart on the prepared cookie sheets.

6 Bake until the cookies are just firm to the touch, about 12 minutes. With a slotted spatula, transfer the cookies to a wire rack and let cool.

Cowboy Cookies

MAKES 60

1 cup flour

½ teaspoon baking soda

¼ teaspoon baking powder

¼ teaspoon salt

½ cup (1 stick) butter or margarine, at room temperature

½ cup granulated sugar

½ cup light brown sugar, firmly packed

1 egg

½ teaspoon vanilla extract

1 cup rolled oats

1 cup semisweet chocolate chips

1 Preheat the oven to 325°F. Grease 3–4 cookie sheets.

2 Sift the flour, baking soda, baking powder, and salt into a mixing bowl. Set aside.

3 With an electric mixer, cream the butter or margarine and sugars together. Add the egg and vanilla and beat until light and fluffy.

4 ▲ Add the flour mixture and beat on low speed until thoroughly blended. Stir in the rolled oats and chocolate chips, mixing well with a wooden spoon. The dough should be crumbly.

5 ▲ Drop by heaping teaspoonfuls onto the prepared cookie sheets, spacing the cookies about 1 inch apart. Bake until just firm around the edge but still soft to the touch in the center, about 15 minutes. With a slotted spatula, transfer the cookies to a wire rack and let cool.

Gingersnaps (top), Cowboy Cookies

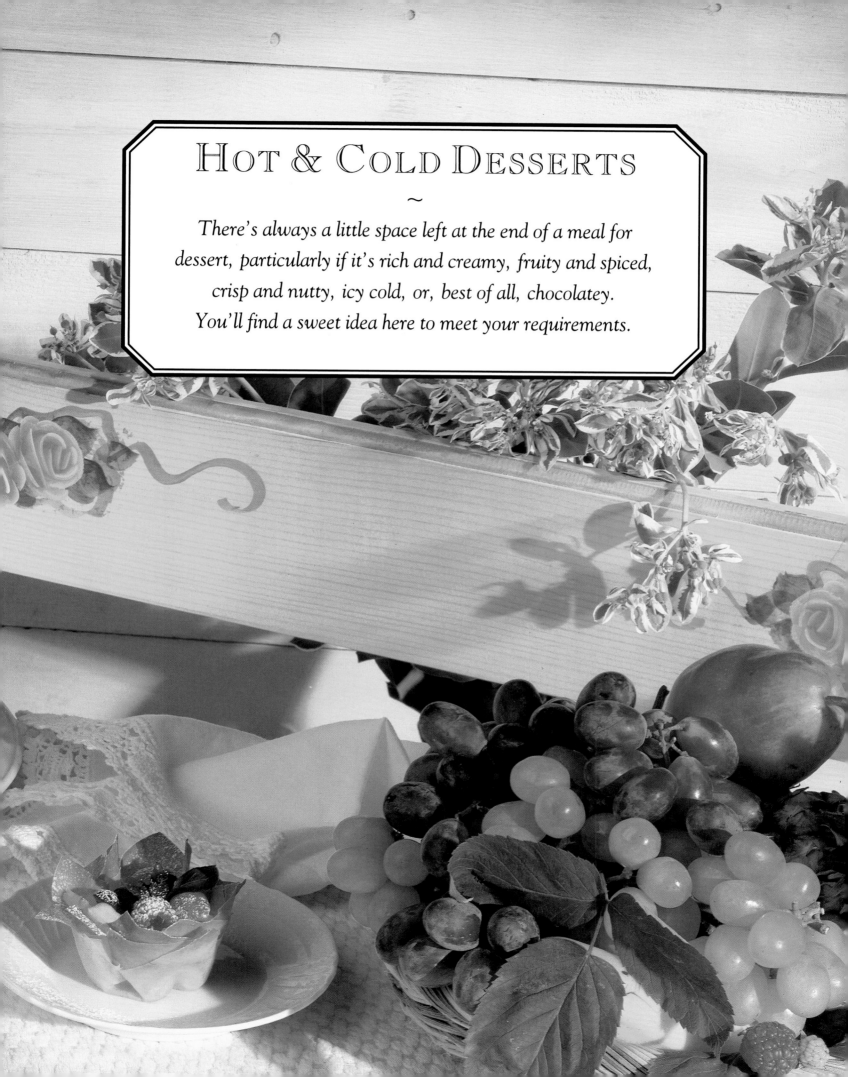

HOT & COLD DESSERTS

~

*There's always a little space left at the end of a meal for
dessert, particularly if it's rich and creamy, fruity and spiced,
crisp and nutty, icy cold, or, best of all, chocolatey.
You'll find a sweet idea here to meet your requirements.*

Baked Apples with Caramel Sauce

SERVES 6

3 Granny Smith apples, cored but not peeled

3 Red Delicious apples, cored but not peeled

¾ cup light brown sugar, firmly packed

¾ cup water

½ teaspoon grated nutmeg

¼ teaspoon freshly ground black pepper

¼ cup walnut pieces

¼ cup golden raisins

4 tablespoons butter or margarine, diced

FOR THE CARAMEL SAUCE

1 tablespoon butter or margarine

½ cup whipping cream

1 Preheat the oven to 375°F. Grease a baking pan just large enough to hold the apples.

2 ▲ With a small knife, cut at an angle to enlarge the core opening at the stem-end of each apple to about 1 inch in diameter. (The opening should resemble a funnel in shape.)

~ **VARIATION** ~

Use a mixture of firm red and gold pears instead of the apples, preparing them the same way. Cook for 10 minutes longer.

---

3 ▲ Arrange the apples in the prepared pan, stem-end up.

4 ▲ In a small saucepan, combine the brown sugar, water, nutmeg, and pepper. Bring the mixture to a boil, stirring. Boil for 6 minutes.

5 ▲ Mix together the walnuts and golden raisins. Spoon some of the walnut-raisin mixture into the opening in each apple.

6 ▲ Top each apple with some of the diced butter or margarine.

7 ▲ Spoon the brown sugar sauce over and around the apples. Bake, basting occasionally with the sauce, until the apples are just tender, about 50 minutes. Transfer the apples to a serving dish, reserving the brown sugar sauce in the baking dish. Keep the apples warm.

8 ▲ For the caramel sauce, mix the butter or margarine, cream, and reserved brown sugar sauce in a saucepan. Bring to a boil, stirring occasionally, and simmer until thickened, about 2 minutes. Let the sauce cool slightly before serving.

Upside-Down Pear Brownies

SERVES 8

½ cup flour

1 teaspoon baking powder

¼ teaspoon salt

7 1-ounce squares semisweet chocolate

½ cup (1 stick) butter or margarine

2 eggs

½ cup sugar

½ teaspoon vanilla extract

1 tablespoon strong black coffee

¼ cup semisweet chocolate chips

½ cup walnut pieces, chopped

1½ pounds ripe pears, or 2 14-ounce cans pear quarters, drained

1 Preheat the oven to 375°F. Grease a 9-inch round nonstick baking dish.

2 Sift the flour, baking powder, and salt into a small bowl. Set aside.

3 In a heatproof bowl set over a pan of simmering water, or in a double boiler, melt the chocolate and butter or margarine. Remove the bowl from the heat and let cool slightly.

4 ▲ Beat the eggs, sugar, vanilla, and coffee into the melted chocolate mixture. Stir in the flour mixture, chocolate chips, and walnuts.

5 ▲ If using fresh pears, peel, quarter, and core them. Arrange the pear quarters in the prepared baking dish, with the rounded ends against the side of the dish. Pour the batter evenly over the pears.

6 Bake 1 hour, covering with foil after 30 minutes. Let cool 15 minutes, then hold an upturned plate tightly over the top of the baking dish, invert and unmold. Serve hot.

Ginger Baked Pears

SERVES 6

6 large firm pears, peeled, cored, and sliced lengthwise

¼ cup honey

¼ cup light brown sugar, firmly packed

1 tablespoon finely grated fresh gingerroot

½ cup whipping cream

1 ▼ Preheat the oven to 400°F. Butter a 10-inch oval gratin dish or shallow baking dish. Fan the pear slices in a spiral design in the bottom of the baking dish.

┌─────────────────────────────┐

~ V ARIATION ~

Substitute firm (even underripe) peaches for the pears. To peel, dip the peaches in boiling water for about a minute, then slip off the skins. Cook as for pears.

└─────────────────────────────┘

2 ▲ In a small bowl, mix together the honey, brown sugar, gingerroot, and cream. Pour this mixture over the pears.

3 Bake until the pears are tender and the top is lightly golden, about 30 minutes. Serve hot.

Upside-Down Pear Brownies (top), Ginger Baked Pears

Blueberry Buckle

SERVES 8

2 cups flour

2 teaspoons baking powder

½ teaspoon salt

½ cup (1 stick) butter or margarine, at room temperature

¾ cup granulated sugar

1 egg

½ teaspoon vanilla extract

¾ cup milk

1 pint fresh blueberries

whipped cream, for serving

FOR THE TOPPING

½ cup light brown sugar, firmly packed

½ cup flour

½ teaspoon salt

½ teaspoon ground allspice

4 tablespoons butter or margarine

2 teaspoons milk

1 teaspoon vanilla extract

1 Preheat the oven to 375°F. Grease a 9-inch round gratin dish or shallow baking dish.

2 Sift the flour, baking powder, and salt into a small bowl. Set aside.

3 ▲ With an electric mixer, or using a wooden spoon, cream together the butter or margarine and granulated sugar. Beat in the egg and vanilla. Add the flour mixture alternately with the milk, beginning and ending with the flour.

4 ▲ Pour the batter into the prepared dish. Sprinkle the blueberries evenly over the batter.

5 ▲ For the topping, combine the brown sugar, flour, salt, and allspice in a bowl. With a pastry blender, cut in the butter or margarine until the mixture resembles coarse crumbs.

6 ▲ Mix together the milk and vanilla. Drizzle over the flour mixture and toss lightly with a fork to mix.

7 Sprinkle the topping over the blueberries. Bake until a cake tester inserted in the center comes out clean, about 45 minutes. Serve warm, with whipped cream if you like.

Peach Cobbler

SERVES 6

5 cups peeled and sliced peaches (about 3 pounds)

3 tablespoons sugar

2 tablespoons peach brandy

1 tablespoon fresh lemon juice

1 tablespoon cornstarch

FOR THE DOUGH

1 cup flour

1½ teaspoons baking powder

¼ teaspoon salt

⅓ cup finely ground almonds

¼ cup plus 1 tablespoon sugar

4 tablespoons butter or margarine

⅓ cup milk

¼ teaspoon almond extract

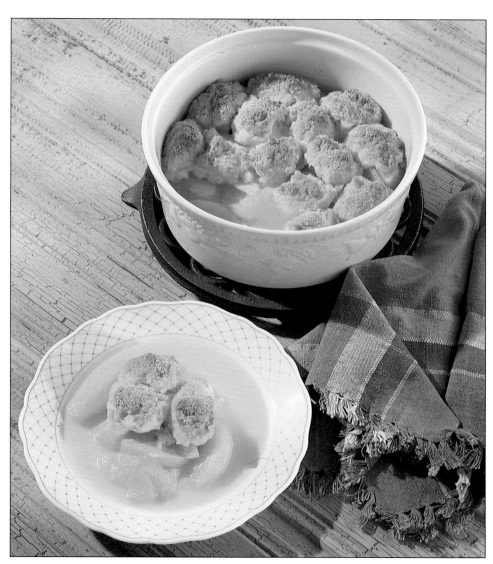

1 Preheat the oven to 425°F.

2 In a bowl, toss the peaches with the sugar, peach brandy, lemon juice, and cornstarch.

3 Spoon the peach mixture into a 2-quart baking dish.

4 ▲ For the dough, sift the flour, baking powder, and salt into a mixing bowl. Stir in the ground almonds and ¼ cup sugar. With 2 knives, or a pastry blender, cut in the butter or margarine until the mixture resembles coarse crumbs.

5 ▼ Add the milk and almond extract and stir until the dough is just combined.

6 ▲ Drop the dough by spoonfuls onto the peaches. Sprinkle with the remaining tablespoon of sugar.

7 Bake until the cobbler topping is browned, 30–35 minutes. Serve hot, with ice cream, if you like.

Rice Pudding with Mixed Berry Sauce

SERVES 6

2 cups short-grain rice
1⅓ cups milk
⅛ teaspoon salt
½ cup light brown sugar, firmly packed
1 teaspoon vanilla extract
2 eggs, beaten
grated rind of 1 lemon
1 teaspoon fresh lemon juice
2 tablespoons butter or margarine
FOR THE SAUCE
½ pint strawberries, hulled and quartered
½ pint raspberries
½ cup granulated sugar
grated rind of 1 lemon

1 Preheat the oven to 325°F. Grease a deep 2-quart baking dish.

2 ▼ Bring a medium saucepan of water to a boil. Add the rice and boil 5 minutes. Drain. Transfer the rice to the prepared baking dish.

3 In a medium bowl, combine the milk, salt, brown sugar, vanilla, eggs, and lemon rind and juice. Pour this mixture over the rice and stir well.

4 ▲ Dot the surface of the rice mixture with the butter or margarine. Bake until the rice is cooked and creamy, about 50 minutes.

5 ▲ Meanwhile, for the sauce, combine the berries and sugar in a small saucepan. Stir over low heat until the sugar dissolves completely and the fruit is becoming pulpy. Transfer to a bowl and stir in the lemon rind. Refrigerate until required.

6 ▲ Remove the rice pudding from the oven. Let cool completely, and serve with the berry sauce.

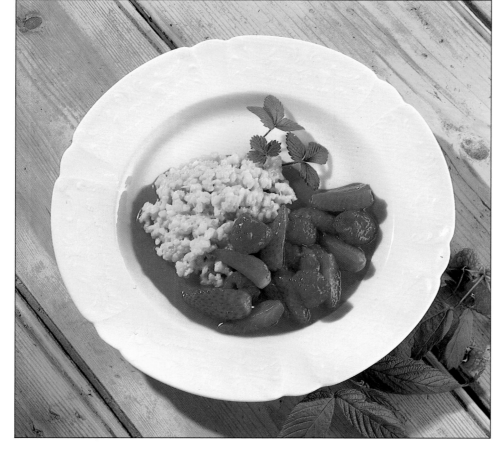

Phyllo Fruit Baskets

SERVES 6

4 large or 8 small sheets of phyllo pastry, thawed if frozen

5 tablespoons butter or margarine, melted

1 cup whipping cream

¼ cup strawberry preserves

1 tablespoon Cointreau or other orange liqueur

1 cup seedless red grapes, halved

1 cup seedless green grapes, halved

1 cup fresh pineapple cubes

½ pint raspberries

2 tablespoons confectioners' sugar

6 small sprigs of fresh mint, for garnishing

1 Preheat the oven to 350°F. Grease 6 cups of a muffin pan.

2 ▲ Stack the phyllo sheets and cut with a sharp knife or scissors into 24 4½-inch squares.

3 ▲ Lay 4 squares of pastry in each of the 6 muffin cups. Press the pastry firmly into the cups, rotating slightly to make star-shaped baskets.

4 ▼ Brush the pastry baskets lightly with butter or margarine. Bake until the pastry is crisp and golden, 5–7 minutes. Let cool on a wire rack.

5 In a bowl, lightly whip the cream until soft peaks form. Gently fold the strawberry preserves and Cointreau into the cream.

6 ▲ Just before serving, spoon a little of the cream mixture into each pastry basket. Top with the fruit. Sprinkle with confectioners' sugar and decorate each basket with a small sprig of mint.

Chocolate Cheesecake

SERVES 12

1 pound (16 1-ounce squares) semisweet chocolate, broken into pieces

½ cup granulated sugar

2 teaspoons vanilla extract

4 eggs

3 8-ounce packages cream cheese, at room temperature

2–3 tablespoons confectioners' sugar, for decoration

FOR THE CRUST

1 cup graham cracker crumbs

5 tablespoons butter or margarine, melted

2 tablespoons grated semisweet chocolate

2 tablespoons granulated sugar

1 ▲ Preheat the oven to 325°F. Grease a 9- or 10-inch springform pan and line the bottom with wax paper. Grease the wax paper.

~ **VARIATION** ~

For an all-chocolate cheesecake, substitute an equal quantity of finely crushed chocolate wafers for the graham cracker crumbs when preparing the crust.

2 ▲ For the crust, mix together the graham cracker crumbs, melted butter or margarine, grated chocolate, and sugar. Pat evenly over the bottom and up the sides of the prepared pan. (The crust will be thin!)

3 ▲ In a heatproof bowl set over a pan of barely simmering water, or in a double boiler, melt the chocolate with the granulated sugar. Remove the bowl from the heat and stir in the vanilla. Let cool briefly.

4 ▲ In another bowl, beat together the eggs and cream cheese until smooth and homogeneous. Gently stir in the cooled chocolate mixture until completely blended.

5 ▲ Pour the chocolate filling into the crumb crust. Bake until the filling is set, 45 minutes.

6 ▲ Let cool, in the pan, on a wire rack. Refrigerate at least 12 hours.

7 ▲ Remove the side of the pan and transfer the cheesecake to a serving plate. To decorate, lay a paper doily on the surface of the cake and sift the confectioners' sugar evenly over the doily. With two hands, carefully lift off the doily.

Chocolate Pudding Cake

SERVES 6

¾ cup flour

2 teaspoons baking powder

⅛ teaspoon salt

4 tablespoons butter or margarine

1 1-ounce square unsweetened
chocolate

½ cup granulated sugar

6 tablespoons milk

¼ teaspoon vanilla extract

whipped cream, for serving

FOR THE TOPPING

2 tablespoons instant coffee

1¼ cups hot water

½ cup dark brown sugar, firmly packed

⅓ cup granulated sugar

2 tablespoons unsweetened cocoa
powder

1 Preheat the oven to 350°F. Grease a 9-inch square baking pan.

2 Sift the flour, baking powder, and salt into a small bowl. Set aside.

3 In a heatproof bowl set over simmering water, or in a double boiler, melt the butter or margarine, chocolate, and granulated sugar, stirring occasionally. Remove the bowl from the heat.

4 ▲ Add the flour mixture and stir well. Stir in the milk and vanilla.

5 ▲ Pour the batter into the prepared baking pan.

6 For the topping, dissolve the coffee in the water. Let cool.

7 ▲ Mix together the sugars and cocoa powder. Sprinkle the mixture over the batter.

8 ▲ Pour the coffee evenly over the surface. Bake 40 minutes. Serve immediately with whipped cream.

Individual Chocolate Soufflés

SERVES 6

5 tablespoons sugar
½ cup plus 1 tablespoon unsweetened cocoa powder
⅓ cup cold water
6 egg whites
confectioners' sugar, for dusting

1 Preheat the oven to 375°F. Lightly butter 6 individual soufflé dishes or ramekins. Mix together 1 tablespoon of sugar and 1 tablespoon of cocoa powder. Sprinkle this mixture over the bottom and sides of the dishes and shake out any excess.

2 ▲ In a saucepan, combine the remaining cocoa powder and the cold water. Bring to a boil over medium heat, whisking constantly. Pour into a mixing bowl.

3 ▲ With an electric mixer, beat the egg whites until soft peaks form. Add the remaining sugar and continue beating until the peaks are stiff.

4 ▼ Add one-quarter of the egg whites to the chocolate mixture and stir well to combine. Add the remaining egg whites and fold gently but thoroughly, until no streaks of white are visible.

5 ▲ Divide the chocolate mixture between the prepared dishes, filling them to the top. Smooth the surface with a metal spatula. Run your thumb around the rim of each dish so the mixture will not stick when rising.

6 Bake until well risen and set, 14–16 minutes. Dust with confectioners' sugar and serve immediately.

Hot Fudge Brownie Sundaes

SERVES 8

1 recipe Hazelnut Brownies (page 221)

1 pint vanilla ice cream

1 pint chocolate ripple ice cream

½ cup walnut pieces, chopped

FOR THE HOT FUDGE SAUCE

3 tablespoons butter or margarine

⅓ cup granulated sugar

⅓ cup dark brown sugar, firmly packed

½ cup unsweetened cocoa powder

⅓ cup whipping cream

⅛ teaspoon salt

1 ▼ For the sauce, combine all the ingredients in a saucepan. Cook gently, stirring, until it is smooth.

2 Cut the brownie cake into squares. Put a brownie in each of 8 bowls.

3 ▼ Top each brownie with a scoop of each ice cream. Spoon the hot fudge sauce on top. Sprinkle with chopped walnuts and serve immediately.

Chocolate Cookie Ice Cream

MAKES 1½ QUARTS

2 cups whipping cream

3 egg yolks

1½ cups sweetened condensed milk

4 teaspoons vanilla extract

1 cup coarsely crushed chocolate sandwich cookies (about 12 cookies)

2 In a mixing bowl, whip the cream until soft peaks form. Set aside.

3 ▼ In another bowl, beat the egg yolks until thick and pale. Stir in the sweetened condensed milk and vanilla. Fold in the cookies and whipped cream.

5 ▲ To serve, remove the ice cream from the pan and peel off the foil. Cut into thin slices with a sharp knife.

1 ▲ Line a 9- × 5-inch loaf pan with foil, leaving enough overhang to cover the top.

4 Pour into the prepared loaf pan. Cover with the foil overhang and freeze until firm, about 6 hours.

~ **COOK'S TIP** ~

Buying very fresh eggs from a reputable producer is especially important when using them raw.

Hot Fudge Brownie Sundaes (top), Chocolate Cookie Ice Cream

Chocolate Mint Ice Cream Pie

SERVES 8

⅔ cup semisweet chocolate chips

3 tablespoons butter or margarine

2 cups crisped rice cereal

1 quart mint-chocolate-chip ice cream

3 1-ounce squares semisweet chocolate

1 Line a 9-inch pie pan with foil. Place a round of wax paper over the foil in the bottom of the pan.

2 In a heatproof bowl set over a pan of barely simmering water, or in a double boiler, melt the chocolate chips and butter or margarine.

3 ▲ Remove the bowl from the heat and gently stir in the cereal, ½ cup at a time. Let cool 5 minutes.

4 ▲ Press the chocolate-cereal mixture evenly over the bottom and up the sides of the prepared pan, forming a ½-inch rim. Refrigerate until completely hard.

5 Carefully remove the crust from the pan and peel off the foil and wax paper. Return the crust to the pie pan.

6 Remove the ice cream from the freezer and let soften 10 minutes at room temperature.

7 ▼ Spread the ice cream evenly in the crust. Freeze until firm, about 1 hour.

8 For the decoration, use the heat of your hands to slightly soften the chocolate squares. Draw the blade of a swivel-headed vegetable peeler along the smooth surface of each chocolate square to shave off short, wide curls. Refrigerate the chocolate curls until needed.

9 ▲ Scatter the chocolate curls over the ice cream just before serving.

INDEX

A

angel food cake, coconut, 92
apples: apple and pear skillet
    cake, 95
  baked apples with caramel
    sauce, 112
  braised red cabbage with
    apples, 76
  pork chop, potato and
    apple scallop, 48
asparagus: asparagus, corn
    and red bell pepper
    quiche, 82
  fried rice with asparagus
    and shrimp, 88
avocado: avocado, grapefruit
    and cantaloupe salad, 66
  chilled avocado and
    zucchini soup, 10
  guacamole cheeseburgers,
    46
  guacamole with cumin
    tortilla chips, 27
  pasta and avocado salad, 70

B

banana cream pie, 99
basil: tomato and basil
    tartlets, 85
beef: chili con carne, 46
  chili dogs, 17
  guacamole cheeseburgers,
    46
  old-fashioned beef stew, 44
  steak, bell pepper and corn
    stir-fry, 45
bell peppers: asparagus, corn
    and red bell pepper
    quiche, 82
  green bean and red bell
    pepper stir-fry, 74
  steak, bell pepper and corn
    stir-fry, 45
black bean and tomato salsa
    in corncups, 20
black-eyed peas and ham
    salad, 71
blueberry buckle, 116
bread: cheesy bread pudding,
    84
  corn bread, 102
broccoli and cauliflower
    mold, 74
brownies: hazelnut brownies,
    105
  hot fudge brownie sundaes,
    124

upside-down pear
    brownies, 114
bulgur wheat salad, 86
burgers: guacamole
    cheeseburgers, 46
  lamb burgers with
    cucumber-mint relish,
    50

C

cabbage: creamy coleslaw, 68
cakes: apple and pear skillet
    cake, 95
  carrot cake with cream
    cheese frosting, 94
  coconut angel food cake,
    92
  devil's food cake, 96
  hazelnut brownies, 105
caramel sauce, baked apples
    with, 112
carrots: carrot cake with
    cream cheese frosting, 94
  glazed carrots and scallions,
    76
cheese: baby baked potatoes
    with blue-cheese
    topping, 26
  broccoli and cauliflower
    mold, 74
  cheese and mushroom
    frittata, 24
  cheesy bread pudding, 84
  green bean and Parmesan
    soup, 12
  guacamole cheeseburgers, 46
  hot cheesy grits, 86
  mozzarella, tomato and
    pesto sandwiches, 14
  spinach and cheese pie, 81
  spinach and feta phyllo
    triangles, 18
cheese, cream: banana cream
    pie, 99
  carrot cake with cream
    cheese frosting, 94
  chocolate cheesecake, 120
cheesecake, chocolate, 120
cherry lattice pie, 100
chicken: barbecue chicken,
    57
chicken breasts with prunes
    and almonds, 54
chicken-noodle soup, 11
chicken thighs wrapped in
    bacon, 60
club sandwiches, 16
deviled chicken

drumsticks, 60
  honey roast chicken, 58
  southern fried chicken,
    55
chili: chili con carne, 46
  chili dogs, 17
chocolate: chocolate
    cheesecake, 120
  chocolate cookie ice
    cream, 124
  chocolate mint ice cream
    pie, 126
  chocolate pudding cake,
    122
  devil's food cake, 96
  five-layer bars, 106
  hazelnut brownies, 105
  hot fudge brownie sundaes,
    124
  individual chocolate
    soufflés, 123
  Mississippi mud pie, 98
  upside-down pear
    brownies, 114
citrus fish fillets, 32
clams: New England
    clambake with lobster,
    40
club sandwiches, 16
cobbler, peach, 117
coconut: coconut angel food
    cake, 92
  five-layer bars, 106
cod: breaded fish with tartare
    sauce, 30
  peppercorn-crusted cod
    steaks, 34
coleslaw, creamy, 68
cookies: chocolate cookie ice
    cream, 124
  cowboy, 108
  gingersnaps, 108
  old-fashioned sugar, 104
  pepper-spice, 106
cool and crunchy salad, 67
corn: asparagus, corn and red
    bell pepper quiche, 82
  corn and garlic fritters, 24
  steak, bell pepper and corn
    stir-fry, 45
Cornish game hens with
    cranberry sauce, 56
cornmeal: corn bread, 102
  cornmeal and smoked
    salmon muffins, 20
  crunchy corn sticks, 102
  hot cheesy grits, 86
cowboy cookies, 108
crab: crab-stuffed cherry

tomatoes, 22
cranberries: Cornish game
    hens with cranberry
    sauce, 56
crunchy corn sticks, 102
cucumber-mint relish, lamb
    burgers with, 50

D

deviled chicken drumsticks,
    60
devil's food cake, 96

E

eggs: cheese and mushroom
    frittata, 24
  Spanish omelet, 80

F

five-layer bars, 106
frittata, cheese and
    mushroom, 24
fritters, corn and garlic, 24

G

ginger: ginger baked pears,
    114
  gingersnaps, 108
grapefruit, avocado and
    cantaloupe salad, 66
green beans: green bean and
    Parmesan soup, 12
  green bean and red bell
    pepper stir-fry, 74
grits, hot cheesy, 86
guacamole cheeseburgers,
    46
guacamole with cumin
    tortilla chips, 27

H

ham and black-eyed pea
    salad, 71
hazelnut brownies, 105
honey roast chicken, 58

I

ice cream: chocolate cookie
    ice cream, 124
  chocolate mint ice cream
    pie, 126
  hot fudge brownie sundaes,
    124

J

jícama: cool and crunchy salad, 67

K

kabobs: glazed lamb kabobs, 50
scallop kabobs, 40

L

lamb: lamb burgers with cucumber-mint relish, 50
glazed lamb kabobs, 50
roast rack of lamb, 53
sesame lamb chops, 52
lentil soup, hearty, 12
lobster, New England clambake with, 40

M

melon: avocado, grapefruit and cantaloupe salad, 66
mint: chocolate mint ice cream pie, 126
Mississippi mud pie, 98
mozzarella, tomato and pesto sandwiches, 14
muffins: cornmeal and smoked salmon, 20
mushrooms: cheese and mushroom frittata, 24
mussels: seafood stew, 39
mustard: pork with mustard-peppercorn sauce, 48

N

New England clambake with lobster, 40
noodles: chicken-noodle soup, 11

O

old-fashioned beef stew, 44
old-fashioned sugar cookies, 104
omelet, Spanish, 80
onions: baked onions with sun-dried tomatoes, 78
cool and crunchy salad, 67
orange: cool and crunchy salad, 67

P

pancakes: potato pancakes with lemon-chive cream, 22
pasta and avocado salad, 70
peach cobbler, 117
pears: apple and pear skillet cake, 95
ginger baked pears, 114
upside-down pear brownies, 114
pepper-spice cookies, 106
pesto: mozzarella, tomato and pesto sandwiches, 14
phyllo fruit baskets, 119
pies: banana cream pie, 99
cherry lattice pie, 100
chocolate mint ice cream pie, 126
Mississippi mud pie, 98
spinach and cheese pie, 81
pita bread: salad-stuffed pita pockets, 14
pork: pork chop, potato and apple scallop, 48
pork with mustard-peppercorn sauce, 48
potatoes: baby baked potatoes with blue-cheese topping, 26
new potatoes with shallot butter, 72
pork chop, potato and apple scallop, 48
potato pancakes with lemon-chive cream, 22
potato salad, 68
scalloped potatoes, 72
Spanish omelet, 80

Q

quiches and flans: asparagus, corn and red bell pepper quiche, 82
tomato and basil tartlets, 85

R

raspberries: rice pudding with mixed berry sauce, 118
red cabbage: braised red cabbage with apples, 76

red kidney beans: chili con carne, 46
chili dogs, 17
red snapper Veracruz, 36
rice: fried rice with asparagus and shrimp, 88
rice pudding with mixed berry sauce, 118
saffron rice, 88

S

saffron rice, 88
salads: avocado, grapefruit and cantaloupe, 66
bulgur wheat, 86
cool and crunchy, 67
creamy coleslaw, 68
ham and black-eyed pea, 71
pasta and avocado, 70
potato, 68
salad-stuffed pita pockets, 14
salmon: salmon steaks with lime butter, 32
sweet and spicy salmon fillets, 34
sandwiches: club, 16
mozzarella, tomato and pesto, 14
scallions: glazed carrots and scallions, 76
scallop kabobs, 40
seafood: seafood and vegetable stir-fry, 38
seafood stew, 39
sesame lamb chops, 52
shrimp: fried rice with asparagus and shrimp, 88
seafood stew, 39
smoked salmon and cornmeal muffins, 20
sole: citrus fish fillets, 32
stuffed sole rolls, 31
soufflés: individual chocolate, 123
soups: chicken-noodle, 11
chilled avocado and zucchini, 10
fresh tomato, 8
green bean and Parmesan, 12
hearty lentil, 12
winter vegetable, 8
southern fried chicken, 55
Spanish omelet, 80
spinach: spinach and cheese

pie, 81
spinach and feta phyllo triangles, 18
steak, bell pepper and corn stir-fry, 45
stews: old-fashioned beef stew, 44
strawberries: rice pudding with mixed berry sauce, 118
sugar cookies, old-fashioned, 104
sundaes, hot fudge brownie, 124

T

tartare sauce, breaded fish with, 30
tartlets, tomato and basil, 85
tomatoes: black bean and tomato salsa in corncups, 20
crab-stuffed cherry tomatoes, 22
fresh tomato soup, 8
mozzarella, tomato and pesto sandwiches, 14
seafood stew, 39
stewed tomatoes, 79
tomato and basil tartlets, 85
tortillas: black bean and tomato salsa in corncups, 20
guacamole with cumin tortilla chips, 27
trout, baked stuffed, 37
turkey: turkey Kiev, 62
turkey scaloppine with lemon and sage, 63

U

upside-down pear brownies, 114

W

walnuts: upside-down pear brownies, 114
winter vegetable soup, 8

Z

zucchini: chilled avocado and zucchini soup, 10